# NOT
# A
# FAIRY TALE

A story of surviving the first
three years of being a stepmom.

A Memoir

## MADDIE LABERGE

## FriesenPress

Suite 300 - 990 Fort St
Victoria, BC, V8V 3K2
Canada

www.friesenpress.com

**Copyright © 2019 by Maddie Laberge**
First Edition — 2019

ISBN
978-1-5255-6048-4 (Hardcover)
978-1-5255-6049-1 (Paperback)
978-1-5255-6050-7 (eBook)

*1. Biography & Autobiography, Personal Memoirs*
*2. Family & Relationships, Parenting, Stepparenting*
*3. Humor, Topic, Marriage & Family*

Distributed to the trade by The Ingram Book Company

*This book is dedicated to any parent who is trying to bend,*
*when they feel like breaking.*

# TABLE OF CONTENTS

# Prologue

I sat on the pirate ship, tipsy amidst the party goers, while the unforgiving sun blazed down on my face. Within twenty-four hours of our arrival in Cabo, a pink hue had surfaced on my skin. With every passing day, I had turned a darker shade of crimson. My body ached. *What was I doing here?*

I watched Biker Nana laugh and dance with the other revelers. She sipped her drink and began singing with the music. In her usual brazen manner, she threw one arm around a pirate's waist and they swayed hip to hip until the song was over.

I glanced over at my partner, Mark. "Your mom is wild."

We both watched her saunter towards the bar and ask for another tequila. The jovial man in the red bandana and matching sash handed her a drink. She winked at him and tossed her blonde highlighted hair over her shoulder as she disappeared back into the party.

Mark gave me that look. "I can't believe she convinced us to come to Mexico."

Only seventeen years older than Mark and a badass in her younger days, Mark's mom Cheryl, or as Mark liked to call her, "Biker Nana," remained edgy and cool. A former exotic dancer, she now took on the role of 'Nana' to seven grandkids: Mark's three and his sister Nicole's four. Cheryl had mellowed out in her personal life, but this tigress never fully changed her stripes. From prowling through the bustling streets and bright lights on the Vegas Strip, to riding her motorcycle across the country, she loved to vacation where the action was.

Cheryl insisted on these yearly family trips to get everyone together for a good time. This year, she planned the fancy Mexican resort, whale watching, Cabo Wabo, and of course the Pirate Ship. Neither Mark nor I could match her sense of adventure. Mark, now mostly a non-drinker, had become more of a homebody and relied on the quiet and calm home environment we had created. He had left his party days behind years ago and followed a predictable routine to strive for a balanced lifestyle. As the pirate ship swayed back and forth, stability was the last thing on our minds.

Even though it could be chaotic, I liked spending time with Mark's whole family, especially when we were able to take his kids with us. This time we took his two older ones; Curtis who was nine years old, and Erin who was seven. Unfortunately, we had to leave James (his youngest) behind with his mother. We admitted that he might not be mentally prepared for this kind of adventure.

I didn't have children of my own; and that was by choice. I enjoyed my freedom and was trying to build a career as a holistic nutritionist. But these were Mark's kids so I always welcomed the opportunity to get to know them better. This was my fourth time spending more than a few days with them.

Our ship adventure got off to a fun start. Erin spent the first hour playing with her cousins, but soon told Mark she needed something to eat. It had not occurred to us to bring any snacks for her or Curtis. *Do parents usually bring treats for their children?* Erin's face soured as she complained of her hunger. Mark asked one of the pirates when they were serving lunch and was told it would be after we went snorkeling, which wasn't for another hour or so. He sat back down with Erin and tried to reason with her.

The pirates slowed the ship to a stop. It was whale watching time. I stood to get a better view while Mark negotiated with Erin. I walked away; Erin was Mark's daughter. I had no idea what to say.

Feeling unable to help when it came to children was familiar to me. It seemed to me that some adults have a built-in intuitive kid compass while I had no confidence on how to navigate their complicated psyches. Scoring well in my psychology classes in university did not translate to an understanding of children. Whenever I tried to interact with them, I acted silly and used humour as the common denominator. They usually stared at me straight-faced or confused, like I was a drunk clown trying too hard. I could read their minds: Fail.

I didn't have success with babies either. I mimicked the behaviour of other women at baby showers, keeping up some sort of charade like I knew what I was doing. When asked if I wanted to hold the baby, I tried to give an award winning performance and gush, "Oh yes! *Of course* I want to hold the baby!" But my scheme was foiled when the infant began shrieking almost immediately after being placed in my tense arms. It was clear I would never be an actress, nor did I have any desire to be a mother.

Being the youngest of four kids in my family didn't help as I was rarely exposed to children. Maybe it was one of the reasons I couldn't understand them. It reached a point where avoidance worked best, but this option was beginning to fade.

After taking a minute to watch for whales and seeing a couple of them off in the distance, I glanced back. Erin was grumpy and still looked like she was sucking on a lemon wedge. She sat with arms crossed while Mark continued talking, in a more animated way now. Every so often he closed his eyes and rubbed his forehead. I knew he was frustrated. The ship moved on and Erin sulked, accepting that there was no snack for her. When she finally re-joined her cousins, I asked Mark how he was doing. He shook his head, slumped back, and gazed out into the ocean.

The hour passed and we neared land. Mark called over to his mom who was engaged in conversation with the other guests. "Hey, Biker Nana, are you going snorkeling? You'll need to start getting ready."

"Oh, Markie! Of course I am." She dismissed this silly question with a wave of her hand.

He looked over at me. "Are *you* going snorkeling?"

I felt the familiar plaguing nervousness in my gut. At a young age I had become frightened of the unknown and this prompted me to say 'no' to new experiences. I spent years letting anxiety and claustrophobia displace the sort of courage one conjures up to feel accomplished and alive. But I worked for months on envisioning this moment. Through some therapy and reading countless books on conquering anxiety, I learned to use visualization as a central coping method to help me take the plunge into waters that I feared.

In the last few months, I imagined everything going smoothly, while I focused on my breathing and relaxing. I conjured up images of my bronzed bikini body gliding through shallow turquoise waters, swimming around pools of tiny fluorescent fish. My soul would feel soothed and I'd float into a fairy tale dream land. I was ready.

I had to be brave and see the snorkeling through. I took a deep breath and seized my gumption. "Yes. I'm doing it." The words sounded strange coming out of my mouth.

Once the boat docked, the pirates gave us instructions on how to secure our life jackets. We worked for a couple of minutes to get Curtis and Erin suited up in the appropriately-sized gear. Curtis could not stand still; his whole body was vibrating as Mark zipped his scuba vest. He had talked about this moment from the first day we arrived.

Once we had our flippers on, they told us to line up. Nicole and her husband—who Curtis and Erin called 'Uncle B'—were a little closer to the front. Their young girls had full smiles and chatted about what it would be like once in the ocean. The line was quite long. I told Mark to stay where he was as I wanted to stand at the end to be the last one in. I didn't want to be in the water longer than I had to.

I couldn't see her from the back of the line, but I heard Biker Nana call out as she jumped in: "Woo Hoo!"

It took a moment to figure out they were getting everyone to walk the plank. *We're jumping off the plank?* I looked out at the water. The drop must have been fifteen feet. A surge of anxiety fluttered in my chest.

The first few people off the plank yelled back that the water was cold. Cold in Mexico? I'm going to walk the plank and fall into frigid water? This didn't sound like the right start to my snorkeling fantasy. I heard someone's child scream from the water. One of the pirates lowered a rope ladder to bring the kid back up, but to my surprise, it wasn't a kid. It was Uncle B— his tall lanky body, soaking wet crawling back onto the ship. His eyes were wide like a scared animal. He scrambled to his feet, shook his head, and put his hands up. "It's not for me! It's not for me! Too cold!" My jaw dropped. If Uncle B couldn't handle the plunge, how was *I* going to?

I was next. I straightened my back and counted on the tequila courage coursing through my veins—which was probably the only courage I had left. I stepped up onto the plank. I didn't come all the way to Mexico to chicken out on the snorkeling. Tiny fluorescent fish awaited my bronzed body's arrival. I stood on the edge looking down at everyone in the water calling me to jump in.

Biker Nana yelled, "You can do it!"

She had a way of making me brave. I plugged my nose and jumped.

Holy shit, COLD! Within seconds I could feel the drop into the crisp ocean clearing out some of the anxiety and liquor-induced cobwebs in my head.

"Swim this way!" I heard the booming voice of the pirate who had leapt into the water first. He pointed to the rocks near the shore. It seemed far. Not being a strong swimmer, I felt especially awkward wearing the flippers and mask, but I swam as fast as I could to stay with the crowd. Curtis was at the front of the pack, even ahead of the guiding pirate. Mark called for him to stay closer, but his little arms and legs were going at maximum speed. Biker Nana swam ahead to catch up to him.

As we neared the larger rocks where the fish were supposed to be, one of the older men began hollering, "There's fish here! They're *huge!*" I couldn't tell if it was excitement or concern in his voice. I tightened up my goggles and stuck my head underneath the surface but all I saw was green water with little pieces of ocean debris floating around.

I heard Curtis shriek, "One hit me in the face!"

*Oh my God, how big are these fish?* He thrashed around for a moment, continued screaming, and then cut back through the crowd of swimmers to make his return to the pirate ship. Biker Nana watched Curtis panic and flee. With a tilt of her head and a sigh of surrender, she took on her Nana duties and called out that she would escort him back.

I could see a panicked Erin trying to crawl onto Mark's shoulders. "Erin, I can't swim with you on top of me!" He eased her off him and stayed beside her as she whined and kicked her flippers to move forward.

Some of the youngsters in the group appeared stunned and began crying as they watched Curtis continue to make his flailing getaway. "I'm scared!" a few of them shouted.

Mark's sister Nicole began laughing, "It's okay. It's fun! It's funny! Ha ha ha!" She glanced at me for support, but I couldn't think of anything, so she continued urging them on. "It's fun you guys! Keep swimming!" I watched Nicole coax the children in the group into renewed enthusiasm. It never occurred to me to handle the situation like that. Her intuitive kid compass had a few years on it and seemed to work great.

Mark called out from a distance behind me, "I'm taking Erin back."

I moved on. It was time to snorkel. I dunked my head in and out. I could see some fish, the size of a foot or so, moving off in my peripheral vision. The water was still somewhat murky and deep, and nothing was glowing. I jerked my body back and forth, desperate to see something that was going to resemble my fantasy. Where were the tiny fluorescent fish hiding? And why was this water still so damn cold?

After a few minutes, many in the group lost interest and started the long swim back to the ship. Soon there was only a handful of us left snorkeling. A teenage girl complained to the pirate, "This is it?" I glanced over thinking the same thing. We all stared at the pirate for an answer. He looked at the few of us and seemed reluctant to speak. "Okay, okay. I'll take you to The Brain, but it's a bit of a further swim." I glanced at the others with new-found excitement.

We swam for another minute or so when he told us to look in the water. Under the surface and a little deeper down was a huge coral ball. We all swam around 'The Brain'. Although it was brown in colour and no fancy fish swam near us, it was unique in its own way and it made me feel like the pirate had told me a secret. He watched us explore it. When he saw grins on our faces, he appeared to breathe a sigh of relief. We headed back to the ship.

By this time almost everyone else had changed back into dry clothing and were guzzling fresh drinks decorated with umbrellas and cherries. Many danced to loud Spanish music while others chowed down on hotdogs.

As Mark was helping me remove my lifejacket, Biker Nana walked over to us.

She raised her hotdog up in front of our faces. "I paid all this money and all I get is this fucking cold wiener." She chomped it and shook her head. Cheryl was a vegetarian.

She began walking away towards the bar then turned back to me, "You did good out there."

She knew how much it took out of me to be adventurous. I appreciated her words.

Mark handed my wet gear to a pirate. "What a disaster. Erin almost drowned me." He raised an eyebrow. "But you guys were out there for a while."

"It's too bad you had to swim back to the boat. It was actually pretty cool; they took us to some coral called The Brain. Maybe we'll come back here and go snorkeling again." We both laughed. We knew we were never coming back here.

Down the narrow stairway was a tiny bathroom below deck where I changed and freshened up. I stared at myself in the mirror. The goggle imprints surrounding my eyes ran deep into my sunburned face, now a new tint of ruby red. I was a little confused and exhausted. I looked the way I felt. I shook my head and laughed. This was far from the fantasy I visualized.

On the sail back, Mark and I were grateful that we were almost finished. Erin and Curtis were now fed, and they danced and played games the pirates set up. I watched the circus continue to unfold around me, numbing myself even further with another lemonade-flavoured Tequila cocktail.

Pictures from that trip show us dancing, singing, swimming, and having a great time. As with most photos of me, none of the internal turbulence I felt was captured. Maybe I was a better actress than I thought.

# Chapter 1

# ERIN

Almost two years after our Mexico trip, Mark and I flew to Vancouver Island.

While the plane descended into Comox airport, Mark opened the window shade. I removed my earbuds and leaned forward to see out. As always, a feeling of peace washed over me as I admired the beauty of the endless towering western red cedars and the thick Douglas firs that welcomed us.

The airport was small and only a few people were travelling on Christmas Day. Instead of the usual hustle upon landing, time seemed to slow to a crawl. We walked out the doors and a quiet cool dampness hung in the air. The green landscape and average coldest temperature of -2 degrees Celsius was something I looked forward to, considering we lived in Edmonton where heaps of snow and heavy, padded coats were the norm during these winter months. I took a moment to breathe it in. Mark loaded my luggage into his mom's truck.

We drove down The Island Highway. Mark sat in the front with his mom, Cheryl, at the wheel. In the back, listening to her stories, I gazed out the side windows for glimpses of the Pacific Ocean and any wildlife. Mother Nature showed off here, and the prairie girl in me was always struck by the alluring scenery. It was so different from the familiar fields of bright yellow sunflowers where I grew up, but so fascinating in its own way. The smaller homes that were nestled off the highway hinted at a simpler life, creating a longing in my soul, a longing that always happened when I visited (what we simply called) the Island. I had never lived here, but nostalgia for my childhood, and the acreage where I spent so many years, always surfaced. A predictable melancholy settled in as I fell into a trance, quietly sitting back as we continued down the winding highway.

Throughout the four and a half years of our relationship, Mark spent all of his vacation time flying or driving out to visit his kids. When possible, I accompanied him. We picked them up and spent four or five days with them at a time. Often we stayed at Cheryl's home, and other times we stayed in hotels that had a swimming pool we could all enjoy. Last year, we had flown the older two out to us for a few weeks in the summer.

Vancouver Island held few surprises now. In addition to visiting the kids over the years, I had taken advantage of the Island's culture. Cheryl and I had toured a few wineries that span the 460 km length of the Island. Maybe seeing the world's largest hockey stick in the city of Duncan wasn't a thrill for me, but the world's largest totem pole in the capital city of Victoria took my breath away. I always felt that the many retirees, Indigenous people, and hippie-like folks that resided on this temperate island, kept the overall pace relaxed and easy going.

Mark's children lived in the south of the Island and Cheryl lived in the middle. We knew we were too far away from them. During last year's summer visit with Erin and Curtis, Mark and I came up with a desperate plan. We decided it was best to figure out how to uproot our life, change provinces and move closer to help raise the children half the time. This was a tough decision from a technical standpoint. We could not imagine where we would work as Mark knew his work in industrial sales wasn't prominent there. I didn't have any savings and he was still getting out of debt from a couple of years of ill-managed finances and a car accident. We decided to make it work somehow. In the end it didn't matter, because when Mark told his ex-wife our plan to move there and help, she told him she'd move away. With her habit of frequently moving, we believed her. She told Mark it would bother her to see us together as a couple and she didn't want me to have anything to do with the kids. She had dragged out the divorce as long as she could, doing whatever she could to avoid being served with the court papers. She told Mark she wanted him to keep paying her the same amount of child support and she knew if he was hired for a new job that paid less, she would also receive less from him. So, we didn't move.

This trip was going to be different, though. Mark and his ex-wife had negotiated a new deal. Erin, was coming back to live with us in Alberta. Curtis and James, Mark's sons, would stay with their mother. Mark and I had been working on this for years. We thought the time would never come. A month earlier, I overheard Erin's excitement during the phone call when Mark relayed the news that we'd be taking her home with us after this Christmas visit.

Mark planned to get the children the next day; tonight, we enjoyed a delicious meal that Cheryl made to celebrate the holiday. The sun set early. We ate by candlelight in her small loft while her black cat slept in front of the fireplace. With a medley of vintage Christmas music playing quietly, we relaxed at her round kitchen table. Cheryl poured some wine while we caught up.

"I'm so happy you're taking Erin. You still have to work on getting the boys, though. They should all be with you; I can't believe she still has them." Cheryl had a visible disdain for Mark's ex-wife when she talked about her. Their once happy and accepting relationship had now turned into a few years of mutual emotional punishment: one regularly launching dreadful accusations at the other. Cheryl believed Mark's ex-wife was a drug addict and only cared about who she could use for money. Cheryl said that the only way she sustained a relationship with Curtis, Erin, and James was through paying. The ex-wife regularly asked for help to pay rent, insurance, phone bills, and groceries. In return, Cheryl was able to visit her grandkids regularly. Cheryl pursed her lips. "That's all she cares about." These stories were nothing new, so as numb as I was to them, I always wished they weren't true. Mark didn't like reminiscing about the past. "I can't change it. I can only move forward," he often said. A part of me knew that a big shift in all of our lives was about to happen. We both wanted to focus on that.

The next day Mark left early and came back at noon with the kids. They opened their presents, then Mark spent an hour tickling and wrestling with them. Giggles filled the air. I watched him raise Curtis in the air and body slam him onto the pull-out couch. "Me next!" they all shouted while he threw each one of them like a sack of potatoes onto the soft mattress.

The visits always started out with a lot of excitement, but the following days were a routine we had adopted on all of our trips here. We washed all their smoky smelling clothing, went into town to get them haircuts, and bought them some new shoes.

While we were out shopping, Erin and I waited in the car for Mark and the boys to finish up in a public washroom. I turned to her.

"Are you excited to move?" I asked.

She nodded and smiled a little as she fixed her gaze out her side window. "Maddie, one time, we went somewhere and my mom made me pee in a cup. Then she told me to pretend it was hers."

"Hmmm. That's weird," I kept my face neutral. "I'm glad you're coming to live with us." I sat back in my seat without knowing what else to say. I was continually disturbed by the unexpected jarring clips of stories I heard. I felt like Erin was waiting for a reaction from me, that even at her young age she recognized that what she told me was significant. We held the silence while waiting a few minutes for Mark and the boys to return.

Every visit with the kids had a turning point where it became awkward. It had been nearly two years since we were in Mexico; Curtis and Erin were now ten and eight, respectively. For some reason they treated and spoke to their younger brother James like a baby. Although James was seven years old, we could barely understand his words and Curtis and Erin spoke for him any chance they had. When we offered James some chocolate ice cream, Erin piped up anxiously, "James doesn't like that."

Mark responded, "He doesn't like chocolate ice cream?"

"Well, I don't think he's ever tried it," she replied.

It turned out James liked chocolate ice cream just fine.

A few days into our trip, Cheryl watched the children so that Mark and I could go on a hike together. We liked to spend time at Englishman River Falls, a popular tourist attraction. A footbridge guided visitors to walk over a rushing waterfall. Once across, lush trails in all directions opened up, waiting to be explored.

We arrived for our hike and I shut the truck door behind me, wrapping my favorite blue scarf around my neck. The air held a cool mist and I stopped for a moment to embrace the forest with my eyes. It rarely snowed on the Island, but it had been a rainy season. The leaves and trees were damp and their greens were dark and deep. It was such a different environment than Alberta where we now lived, or Manitoba where I grew up. Mark reached for my hand as we walked down the uneven terrain.

A few minutes after we crossed the footbridge we noticed the gray clouds in the sky. Small drops of rain tapped my forehead. We continued in silence for a few minutes, not wanting to have to end the hike prematurely.

Mark sighed as he glanced around. "This place, this island, it's so beautiful. But I have so many bad memories here. It feels haunted."

The haunting included a failed marriage followed by a messy separation and divorce that involved many lapses in good judgement. I knew that deep-seated regret lingered within him and began to stir whenever we were here. It had not been easy for either of us, but he had worked hard and turned his life around since we met and formed our relationship. Despite the patience and insight he developed, something in him always reverted when we were on this island. As the days moved into one another, I watched him become more uncomfortable, and eventually, his unease felt contagious. In this land of striking beauty, our visits were always shadowed by Mark's past.

After our hike we stopped at the local gas station to get a coffee fix and fill up the tank. The ocean was across from us. I watched the motion of it, trying to figure out if the tide was coming in or going out. It was raining harder now and the fast-moving clouds felt ominous. The cold wind scooped up the water, throwing waves hard onto the sand. I shivered and wrapped my cold hands around the hot paper cup. Only a few more days and we would be back home.

We boarded the plane late on New Year's Eve. Mark was double checking

Erin's seatbelt when the flight attendant came by. She asked if we were settled in. Erin proclaimed, "I'm going to live in Alberta!" Even though it was a late flight, she dangled her legs back and forth full of energy. I sat back and thought about what my future would look like.

The flight was uneventful. The plane landed and we reached for our luggage overhead. Within a few minutes everyone was standing in the aisle waiting for the door to open. Erin stood patiently between Mark and me. The pilot spoke: "This is your captain speaking with a quick final announcement: The clock is about to hit midnight. Happy New Year, everyone." We all turned to one another with shy smiles and nodded as we wished other passengers a happy new year. A couple of cheers came from the back. Mark and I gave each other a little kiss as we heard the airplane door open. This year would be an adventure.

After the drive home, Mark rolled our luggage into our apartment and I placed Erin's two old grey suitcases on the floor. Mark went to unpack. Erin and I settled in on the couch. She looked up at me with her big brown eyes and short messy brown hair.

"What did you do for fun when you were a kid?"

I thought for a moment before answering. "I used to climb trees."

"Climb trees?"

"Yep. Lots of trees. Do you climb trees?"

"We're not allowed."

"Who says?" Naively, I believed this was something kids were still free and encouraged to do.

"What did you do in the trees?"

"I sat and thought about things."

"What kind of things?"

"Like how beautiful the other trees were, or how good the country air smelled."

I could see she was listening to me, so I continued.

"I had to find ways to climb the bigger trees; sometimes I had to set up our old ladder to reach the first branch. It was hard to get down if I climbed up too far. We also had a tree right beside our house. We'd climb it to get on the roof and walk around on our little home. In the winter we'd gather up huge piles of snow and jump off into them."

Her eyes widened a little. "Your mom and dad let you do that?"

"Yeah. I guess that sounds a little crazy now. But they let us."

"Did you ever fall out of a tree and hurt yourself?"

"Probably. I don't remember. What do you like to do?"

She shrugged, "I don't know."

"I guess we'll figure it out together. Happy New Year, Erin."

"Happy New Year, Maddie."

Having Erin in our home made it real. All of a sudden, I felt a little nervous. I thought about my lack of parenting skills. Did I have any at all? Bigger questions went off like fireworks in my mind: What had happened, or didn't happen that led me to today?

*****

By the time I was fifteen, my parents had already been divorced for five years and my siblings lived elsewhere, so I became an 'only child' of sorts. My mom spent a lot of time with her new husband. They tried to include me in some of their outings and sometimes I went with them to make my mother happy. I didn't find their road trips much fun and my stepdad complained about the food or service at nearly every restaurant. Eventually I told them I preferred to stay home alone.

I had a lot of friends, but I felt lonely for many years. Like most teenagers, I was trying to find my identity and get a sense of the world around me. As I moved through these years, I became angry: at my parents, at the imbalance in justice I began to see. Nothing seemed fair, and as a teenager 'fair' still meant something. I spent years believing if I prayed enough and treated people the way I wanted to be treated, that it would somehow be the measure of how much fairness would return to me. When was the moment in my life that I gave up on the idea of 'fairness' as an expected result?

My upbringing in the church and belief in the Catholic faith faltered in my teen years. Angry with a religion that I was made to believe would give me peace, led to giving up my belief. I don't remember what prompted me in the moment, but on a dark autumn night, I walked out of a house party. I wandered to the far back of the property where I knew a creek ran through. I remember unlatching my silver crucifix necklace. Without ceremony, I threw it in the cold water that ran over the rocks. I was done. I never told anyone. Abandoning the faith almost seemed easy, even a relief, as though instead of relying on God for answers, I would toughen up and accept that many questions don't have answers.

I turned seventeen and searched for other outlets to find comfort. I acquired a few habits that I figured could remedy some of my problems: smoking and drinking, but those only caused mornings of hangovers. I was riddled with anxiety under a thick layer of guilt. I moved in with my boyfriend and dropped out of school. What an aimless disaster I was.

What I didn't see until my thirties was that my anxiety disorder manifested when I 'toughened up'. All those years ago I had abandoned my black-beaded rosary from my First Communion and turned my back on any faith, out of bitterness and frustration. But I replaced it with nothing. I dug a void. It took a long time to realize that there were more options for meditation and answers out there. Even though the church I attended as a child was beautiful, I didn't need to be kneeling in a building of bibles and vibrant stained glass to believe in a creator.

The anxiety I had developed in those teen years became much more substantial once I reached my twenties. It persisted and became nearly unbearable. Panic attacks lurked around corners and waited to jump out at me. I decided something was wrong; something was missing. After working different part-time jobs and essentially standing still in life, I found myself without many life skills or direction. I stumbled around and lived in a few different places, before deciding to move back in with my mom and stepdad. They encouraged me to figure out a plan. During this time my stepdad and I formed a more mature relationship.

He joked, "It only took you ten years to realize I have a sense of humour."

"It only took you ten years to get one," I said.

We laughed a lot together then. I could feel that something had switched over, and our interactions were more meaningful. I gave him Father's Day cards that expressed my gratitude for having him in my life. He stepped up as a dad I could rely on. He gave me solid advice, and encouraged me to explore the idea of pursuing a career.

My mom regularly purchased self-help books from second-hand stores. Her bookshelves were full of them. When I walked into the kitchen for breakfast, she often had a book in her hand and looked up at me. "Oh sit down. I want to read you something." She read a paragraph that she had underlined, and then look at me like she had discovered a diamond. "What do you think of that?"

I have to admit that at times it opened up philosophical conversations that could last for hours.

I was now suffering from unknown fears and searching for purpose, and these books seemed like they could lead me to some answers. I frequently found myself standing in front of my mom's shelves and pulling books off, plopping myself down right there on the carpet in the hallway while I flipped through the chapters. *Love*, by Leo Buscaglia had me hooked. As a poet and thinker, he opened up my young mind to new ideas.

Inspired to make something meaningful out of my life, I took my rediscovered love of reading and turned back to education. My stepdad recommended I attend university. He was the only person who told me I could go. No one else had even suggested it. Eventually I enrolled at the University of Manitoba and earned a degree in Human Nutritional Sciences.

By the time I reached my late twenties, I was living a different life. I had graduated from school and transformed myself from a party-goer into an introvert. I moved back to the small town I grew up in, and became satisfied with listening to some good music, indulging in a glass of wine, and sitting around a bonfire with a friend or two. My life seemed destined for a low-maintenance, country-living existence with the loudest sound being the orchestra of crickets outside my window. I was devoted to watching the stars and counted on the Big Dipper every night for dependable company. I even hung blue Christmas lights outside of my home, keeping them lit year round.

This was it. I had it all figured out. I had left behind my hectic city life and embraced my new-found peace. Around this time, Facebook appeared and I signed up. It began prompting easy digital reunions. Through a series of connections, I stumbled upon a familiar face from fifteen years earlier.

Mark and I had met through mutual friends when we were both fourteen. We spent two days getting to know one another all those years ago while he was in Winnipeg for a short visit. The first day the bunch of us crammed into a booth and ate burgers and fries at a popular joint called, *George's*. The next day we all jumped on a bus to St. Vital mall and saw the movie *Beetlejuice*. Afterwards, Mark and I branched off and talked while we strode around in my neighbourhood during that warm summer night. The time went by fast while we laughed and asked meaningful questions about each other's lives. As dawn broke, he walked me home. We sat together on the cement step in front of my apartment block on St. Anne's Road. I wore his jacket while smoking menthol cigarettes and he rested his head on my lap. I waited as long as I could before announcing I had better sneak back into my room before my mom woke-up. We hugged goodbye and he insisted I keep his jacket to remember him.

Once he was back in Edmonton, he wrote me letters for a year. Our contact tapered off after that and we both moved on with our lives.

Now, through the same mutual friends, I saw his name in my newsfeed.

I sent him a message: "Do you remember me?"

His answer came back almost immediately: "Of course I do."

I couldn't have imagined, now in my mid-thirties, that I would be living in an apartment in Edmonton with him, much less sitting on a couch chatting with my stepdaughter. Erin didn't know any of these things about me. But there we were, beginning to get to know each other, celebrating our first New Year's together.

# Chapter 2

# BROWNIES

Before we brought Erin home, Mark and I had talked about what kind of life we wanted to provide for her. Like most parents, we wanted her to have more than we did. In these discussions we sometimes picked at old scabs about our childhood.

Mark often recalled being in elementary school and seeing the unpaid stack of brown enveloped bills piling up. He wondered how long until the power was turned off this time. He had memories of his mom, Biker Nana, going on the road to pursue her career as an exotic dancer, which she excelled at. This meant she was a feature dancer in many cities. Unfortunately for Mark, her work created not only physical distance, but emotional distance from her as well.

I had my own stories of childhood struggle, though of a different variety to be sure. Like the one about the chocolate-coloured corduroy dress my parents made me wear to my First Communion. In a sea of little girls in white delicate gowns, I felt like a big brown walrus, shuffling along with my head down, praying to go unnoticed.

In some ways we were able to laugh at all of these experiences, even admitting that these events built some character. At the same time, we didn't want Erin to have to build character in the same ways we did.

Mark and I had dissimilar childhoods; he was a city boy and I was from the country. I grew up in a small town in Manitoba where the mercury often dipped below -30 degrees Celsius during the winter. I remember my seven-year-old self and my three older siblings getting ready for school. After making breakfast and sending my dad off with a hot coffee, my mom began the lengthy task of bundling me up. It was the standard gear for those dark months on the prairies: long johns under my pants, then a series of external layers to prevent Old Man Winter's wrath. On these blustering mornings, I was swaddled and padded so tight I could barely move or see out from the scarf wrapped around my head. I grabbed at my school bag with oversized wool mittens and shuffled out the door following my faster sisters, and brother. The padding in my snowsuit was so puffy that I imagine I looked like a bowling ball, stumbling and zig zagging down our long driveway in my bulky hand-me-down winter boots as I hurried to the bus.

Once the bell rang and we were allowed into the school, my classmates and I stripped off our layers of winter armour. When I removed my toque, some of my long blond hair stood straight up, full of static. I cupped my ears with my hands, which weren't much warmer, to bring them back to room temperature as I took a seat at my desk.

My siblings and I made the most of the dramatic winter. Feeling invincible, we used shovels to pile up mountains of snow, then jumped off our old barn, or house, into them. We had a few bumps and bruises, but I don't recall anyone being seriously hurt. Other days, the four of us dragged our two crazy carpets and one toboggan while trudging to the small bridge near our house where there was a hill. We took turns and learned the fine art of sharing early on. If we invited others to come along, we used a large grey shovel made of galvanized sheet metal as a sled. Some of our friends called it dangerous; we thought we were innovative.

My older brother, John, built intricate snow forts that he worked on well into the darkness of the night. Once done, he allowed the rest of us to crawl inside to where he had made shelves in the walls, filled with glowing candles and a lantern.

We all played well into the night. It was easy to do when the stars and moonlight shone down so bright. Some evenings I stayed out so late that when I returned home I could not feel my fingers and toes anymore. Unable, or unwilling, to predict what the weather could do, it wasn't until I was on my knees, reaching out towards our fireplace to warm my hands that the sharp pain of near frostbite set in, tears streaming down my face.

These were the childhood stories that gave me comfort when Mark and I reminisced about them, but I couldn't avoid some of the harder 'character building' ones that swirled into my memories as well.

My parents were dedicated minimalists and for that I'm thankful. This taught me the value of simplicity, but the corresponding lack of opportunities to attend extracurricular activities as a young girl was disheartening. I had the most basic swimming lessons as a child, which as an adult, still kept me hanging onto the sides of the pool or walking on the shore. I was never taught how to ice skate, and I didn't participate in skiing or curling—all winter activities that could have come in handy while riding out the long cold months through my adolescent years. My friends were often enrolled in dance, sports clubs, or summer camps. They asked if I could join, too. My parents *never* encouraged us to do anything that took us too far away from our home. There wasn't an abundance of money coming in since my dad changed jobs so often, and with his regular donation to the church every week, there was even less to go around.

When I mentioned something that I was interested in joining, my mom smiled and nodded while I explained; then she ended the conversation by scrunching up her face a little while saying, "You don't really want to do that, do you?" Or at best I was told, "Well, maybe we'll look into doing that another time." It didn't take me long to stop getting my hopes up.

At one point I decided not to show my parents a permission slip for a school field trip: a play that we would attend in the city. I believed we were better off not spending. The teacher asked me about the form when I had not handed it in, and although the memory is vague, I recall looking down at the floor when questioned, repeating that I didn't want to go. I don't know what conversation took place between that teacher and my parents, but I attended. I remember feeling lucky and having a good time on that outing.

There was one thing, however, I didn't let go of and begged for all the time: to let me join Brownies with my friends. It felt like a miracle because somehow, I convinced them; they even enrolled my sister Jennifer—who was three years older than me—in Girl Guides. My parents never bought us uniforms during that time, but I *did* get a brown sash to wear over my white hand-me-down blouse. I displayed that sash across my torso like a preening peacock as I earned badges. Jennifer and I lasted two or three months before our parents pulled us out. The other girls asked why I had to leave but I didn't know the reason and I could see that they didn't quite understand that not all kids got the same options. "It doesn't mean that much to you, does it?" my mom said as she picked us up after our final meeting.

I went back to solo adventures and sports. I was a fast runner and won several ribbons in track and field events while in elementary school, at a time when there was no such thing as 'participation awards'.

I loved summers in our big yard too. The long days surrounded me with a full sun and high temperatures, which kept me comfortable since I was always so skinny and cold. It was perfect for setting up the old ladder and climbing tall oaks or exploring the loft of the barn. I could swing for hours on the homemade swing set my dad built us or play with my toys in the sandbox. When I wasn't off on my own, there were times that my dad, Jennifer, and I walked the entire tree line. This was a path along the back of our property where we had planted small spruce trees and watched them grow taller every year. Watching those trees inch up was an exercise in patience. I listened to my dad as he talked about nature and I admired his relaxed demeanour in those days.

These adventures didn't cost a penny. Although I created a lot of fun for myself as a kid, I remember the sting of loneliness and of feeling far away from my friends. I wanted more for Erin.

*****

For the first couple of nights that Erin was with us, she felt a little home-sick and talked about missing her brothers, but she was also adapting at a rapid pace. We enrolled her in the same school as her cousins and she made new friends. When I announced she would start attending Brownies the next week, her eyes lit up. I may not have had my chance, but I felt like Erin deserved to have some fun. I didn't know how to parent, but I figured if I gave her things that I wanted as a kid, maybe that would make me a good stepmom.

The women who ran the program were referred to as 'Guiders'. I decided to volunteer and become a Guider myself so that Erin and I could do some bonding. The Brownies met once a week in the basement of Holy Trinity Anglican church. The three Guiders went by owl names. Snowy Owl was clearly the leader. She was a robust woman in her mid-forties, who was gentle with the girls but assertive enough that they respected her. I liked her a lot.

It was our second session now and I adopted the name Cinnamon Owl. Erin bounced around with the other girls as though they had been best friends for years. I, on the other hand, was still trying to make a good impression. I didn't fully understand how they ran the sessions. Not knowing whether I should be doing more or taking some initiative, I stood off to the side and fixed my mouth in a fake grin to try to fit in and be approachable. The same actress in me that came to life at baby showers was now appearing at the Brownies meetings. I hoped my acting skills had improved a little.

When our third session came around, they had me laying out an activity that involved creating paper flowers. Snowy Owl asked if I could go find the construction paper they needed.

The church basement had a creepy—and creaky—door that opened to a dark hallway leading to a supply room. I had to duck so as not to hit my head on a low cement ceiling. I could barely see where I was going but managed to find a larger open space and a hanging string that attached to a single light bulb in the center of the room. I pulled the string and on came a high voltage bulb that illuminated the small cement room like a spotlight. I squinted. There were Christmas decorations overflowing from old cardboard boxes; I could make out a time-worn rickety brown closet near the corner. I climbed over the boxes and opened the old wooden doors and was met with a disastrous shelving unit of mismatched markers, crayons, pencils, paper, tape, and whatever props the church had for their Christmas plays. The nativity statues lined the bottom shelf. *Jesus Christ.* I stood there for a moment adjusting my eyes to take in this mess. I moved items here and there on my quest for the construction paper. I wondered how long it would take to organize. Probably an entire day, maybe two. How could anyone find what they needed here?

I must have been in there a little too long because Snowy Owl appeared under the spotlight.

I looked at her dumbfounded, "I can't find the paper."

She rummaged through the closet, grabbed a handful of the first paper she saw and waved the wad triumphantly in the air, "There we go!"

Confused, I pointed to the paper in her hand, "But that's not construction paper."

"It doesn't matter," she said with a smile while shrugging her shoulders. "Okay, let's go."

I followed her out of the supply room. How was *this* paper going to work?

The Guiders gathered the girls into groups and began directing them on how to cut the paper. But it was too thin and didn't hold the shape of the flowers. I knew it wasn't going to fold up or keep its shape as the construction paper would have. I watched the girls fold and cut and make their designs. As I predicted, their flowers looked awful. I kept thinking about that cluttered and unorganized closet and how if someone had put things in properly, they would be able to find what they needed when they needed it.

But as I walked around the room, I noticed something. All the little girls were laughing. As they giggled, they talked to one another, jumping in place, or running to see what the group beside them was doing. Half of them forgot what they were even working on, nor did they seem to care that their flowers were floppy.

The moment hit me. I was naïve when it came to children and what was important to them. They didn't care about "the correct" anything. They just wanted to have fun. Why didn't I know that? Snowy Owl sure knew it. She was floating around the room having a great time, too. I think I might have felt jealous. Or stupid.

While we cleaned up, I helped put the supplies back into the old closet. I shook my head as I looked at it this time around. I guess I *did* find what I needed in that dingy closet after all.

That session taught me that perfectly planned activities didn't play a large role in that church basement. The point of the Brownies getting together was more about having fun and building relationships. Having the activity come out, 'good enough' was okay. I thought that was what I needed to open my new parenting eyes: an exciting revelation about the psychology of what was important to these girls. But then a few weeks later, Brownies session six came around.

It was "Science Experiment Day". The Owls had different areas set up and they were walking the girls from one experiment to another. Each one failed. Not ONE experiment worked. *Are you kidding me?* I mentally put my face in my palm. I almost choked as I continued to swallow my anxiety for an hour and a half. The worst part was that I knew better. I watched the girls to see if they were having a good time. They were having a blast. They didn't care. Erin was laughing it up with her friends. Why did I care? Why couldn't I have fun through all of this? My dingy closet epiphany from a few weeks earlier was going to take some time to set in.

## SNAPSHOTS

Brownie girl: "Can you show me how to draw a mermaid?"

Me: "Sure!" *draws mermaid*

Brownie girl: "That's Horrible."

Me: "What? Why?"

Brownie girl: "Look at that big chin. That looks like a man."

Me: "Well, here..." *scratches out big chin*

Brownie girl: "You gave him a beard."

# Chapter 3
# SLEEP

Erin had watched the movie *Chucky* sometime before coming to live with us. The movie has a doll that comes to life and terrorizes and kills people. I repeat: The movie. Has a doll named 'Chucky'. That comes to life. And TERRORIZES and KILLS people. Did someone let a six-year-old little girl sit down on a couch with a bowl of popcorn and watch this movie? Or was she peeking behind a corner after bedtime (as children do) and watched it unbeknownst to whoever put it on? I don't know. And it didn't matter. We had to deal with the consequences.

Her nightmares happened almost every night and caused Erin to wake up around 3:00 a.m. We moved her bed right beside ours, hoping to help her feel more secure. It didn't change the pattern. For her first month with us, she woke up her dad. He didn't know what to do. She wanted to sleep *with* us, so without any other solutions, he let her crawl in between us. She eventually dozed off, but with Mark being a restless sleeper to begin with, he was left awake for the rest of the night staring at the ceiling. The sleepless hours started adding up.

One day I went with Mark to drop Erin off at school—a twenty-minute drive. He was maneuvering erratically through traffic while answering his work phone. He stopped at a red light and I glanced at him. I could see the dark circles under his eyes. He gave them a quick rub and dropped some Visine into each one. After a couple of large gulps of his black coffee he stared straight ahead waiting for the light to turn green while mumbling to himself. He didn't even notice me watching him. I knew he only talked to himself when he was stressed and had too many conversations going on at one time in his mind. The light turned green at the same time as his phone rang again. He accelerated and took the call. My concern now turned to anger. Once he was finished the call, I couldn't hold back.

"Can you *not* answer the phone? You're not paying enough attention to the road. I don't feel safe."

He looked at me in a bit of disbelief. "I have to answer it. It's my job."

"Well, not while we're in the car."

A few minutes later it rang again. He didn't answer.

As thankful as we were to have Erin living with us, cracks were forming in our once-strong foundation. Mark and I understood how each other functioned, but navigating full-time parenting with a new schedule was something we were trying to juggle together. What started with a few balls in the air had turned into flaming torches. These were not easy to catch when we were sleep deprived.

Our physical home wasn't ideal. We lived in a one-bedroom rental apartment that didn't allow children under eighteen. When Mark convinced his ex-wife to let us take Erin, we were in the middle of our lease. We hoped but had no idea if we would be able to get the boys anytime soon, so we decided to ride out the last few months in the apartment and hide Erin as best we could so as not to get evicted.

To keep food in the fridge, gas in the tank, and save for a house of our own, Mark and I both worked. To keep his child support up to date, in addition to his day job, Mark still had to bartend on the weekends to pay his ex-wife. The parent who is primarily responsible for their child is eligible to receive a monetary child benefit every month from the government. But at the time, even though Mark was the primary parent for Erin, he was still paying his full support for all three children and we weren't receiving any government cheques. The arrangement that was made to take Erin involved Mark letting the children's mother keep all of the money. This deal had not been made in court as that route wasn't working for us, so Mark had convinced his ex-wife to let us take Erin, under a new agreement, outside the law. It would take until June when the government became involved again.

After a month or so of the dreaded sleep routine, Mark could not take it anymore. He needed some REM sleep. I told him to let Erin wake me up. We had grown closer since we started Brownies. She agreed and felt comfortable with the idea, so from then on I got the 3:00 a.m. Erin wake up-call. She stood over me in the dark room and I felt one finger poke my arm. My first plan was to get out of my bed and go lay down with her on her bed; which was a blow up mattress since our situation in the apartment wasn't permanent. I waited for her to fall back asleep. Sometimes it took ten minutes, sometimes an hour. Because the mattress was so flimsy and the air pockets shifted with any movement, she felt me leave when I tried to slither off it. She sat straight up and we started all over. I imagined that this must be what feedings with a newborn were like. *Please fall asleep.*

After weeks of this, I considered using toothpicks to hold my eyelids open at work. On the odd night that she didn't wake me, I had dreams of her standing over me and reaching out to poke my arm. I opened my eyes often and it kept me from getting into a deep sleep. I needed a different plan. I told her to slide into bed on my side so I could cuddle her and soon we both fell asleep.

Having her own real bed and space was a few months away, which may not sound like a long span, but the uncertainty and stress in our lives caused time to drag. Mark crossed his fingers and I sent out a few prayers to any higher power that would listen. All we could do was try to maintain some stability until we could form a plan to move forward.

# Chapter 4

# NO KIDS ALLOWED

We used the door near the back lane where we were less likely to be spotted. Mark had his key ready to go and Erin was in position to move. Once inside, I tiptoed ahead on the staircase up to the third floor where I peeked beyond another door into the hallway that led straight to our apartment. I looked down the banister as they waited on the second-floor stairs looking up for the signal. "Clear!" I whispered and motioned for them to proceed. We tiptoed down the hallway as fast as we could.

After a couple of months, this routine became more habit than a true fear of getting caught. Most of the time we snickered as it seemed like a big joke to all three of us. Although, when we heard shuffling inside one of the neighbour's door as we passed by, Erin and I looked at one another like a deer in headlights. We knew to make a mad dash to our door, though once in the apartment we giggled without restraint. But the laughter ended when the landlords began sliding maintenance notices under our door.

The owners were an older man and his younger wife who luckily didn't live in the building, so avoiding them was manageable. The wife was a small framed woman who always had on an oversized coat. I guessed she was in her late thirties. I couldn't ignore her beady eyes, jagged teeth, and frizzy hair. She came across as a little rough around the edges and glared at everyone. My interactions with her were as brief as I could make them. Now that Erin lived with us, avoiding this woman wasn't only a preference; we had to keep from being seen or we imagined an eviction notice would show up at any time.

Whenever they wanted to check on anything to fix or update in our apartment, they gave us a three-day window of when they *might* show up. Up until this point, it had not concerned us since Mark and I were often at work whenever they decided to come in. But now we had Erin and her little girl items strewn about the apartment. We could not let anyone come in without being careful to stage the apartment or we'd be busted for sure. Every morning we'd have to deflate Erin's bed, hide all her clothing, toys, and school items before leaving for work. The problem was there were times the landlords didn't show up at all and rescheduled with new 'notices'. This meant that hiding a child became quite a job.

We were becoming paranoid. We were certain that we were going to be found out. The worst thing that could happen would be getting thrown out in the cold weather while we only had a few months left on our lease. If we couldn't sleep before, this new development wasn't helping it get better. The hiding continued.

I was working as a holistic nutritional consultant at the time. One morning after I arrived, a fellow co-worker asked if I could help a customer who was quite distressed. As I walked around the corner, I could see a woman and her baby both crying. I approached her and realized it was my landlord. She glanced up and recognized me. Her eyes were red and she looked so hurt and vulnerable. "My baby is sick. I don't know what else to do." It didn't matter that she was my cranky landlord. I knew I could help her. I asked her to sit down and I talked to her for a while. The tears tapered off as I suggested some ideas and supplements for her sick baby girl. After spending quite a bit of time with her, we exchanged a smile and I gave her a warm pat on the shoulder. "Take care," I said.

When I got home, as usual, Mark was blowing up the air mattress. I told him the story since it was such an odd occurrence. From that day on we stopped getting notices under our door.

## SNAPSHOTS

*Making smoothies with Erin*

Me: "I'm going to add in some lemon fish oil. We'll get some good fatty acids from these."

Erin: "We're gonna get fatty asses?!"

# Chapter 5

# PARTY MOMS

In my late teenage years, I often partied at a bar in the town I grew up in. A group of my close friends worked there and even though I lived in Winnipeg at the time—twenty-five minutes away—I still drove out on Friday nights to catch up on the latest gossip and shoot a few games of pool.

I started out a typical night with a dab of The Body Shop's White Musk rubbed into my wrists and my standard outfit of a tank top and jeans. It wasn't a fancy establishment, but there was often a handful of women who went all out wearing high heels and sultry smiles. Cigarettes—still allowed inside the bars at the time—were perched between most of our fingers. By midnight, the enticing earlier scents of Calvin Klein cologne and sweet words that smelled like breath mints were often replaced with disenchanting hard liquor and harsh language on the tongue. My eyes irritated from smoke and vision blurry from the beer, I glanced around every so often to see a foggy haze and drunk figures mingling. With loud music blaring from the DJ station, we all swirled in nonsensical laughter. What was so funny? It didn't matter. Being young was funny.

The night wore down. Exhausted waitresses and bartenders breathed a sigh of relief and turned on the lights. A few lucky girls and guys exchanged phone numbers. Some of the others who had come with the hope of forgetting their worries ended up visibly distraught as the alcohol turned on them, only magnifying their sober problems. Now at 2:00 a.m., the bouncer shuffled out the stumbling herd.

Beyond the exit doors, it wasn't a surprise to see an overloaded testosterone-fuelled fist fight brewing. That's why the regulars never parked in front of the doors. We all knew some guy might getting pummeled on our car hood.

Cell phones weren't around in any significant way at the time. And it's probably a good thing because, due to the lack of instant Smartphone pictures and messaging, there are minimal recordings of the ridiculous things we did. Without knowing when to shut up in my youth, I shudder when I imagine the emotional vomit that I would have spewed through text messages to crushes or a boyfriend at 3:00 a.m.

Instead, my brain remains the primary storage of data from those crazy Fridays. As the years have passed, my limbic system has developed a few 'viruses', so even the memories I think I'm sure of, can be glitchy. Reminiscing with old friends reveals skewed details of our good times and mis-adventures. Conflicting stories get juggled through the air in between fits of laughter while we try to connect the dots from those days so long ago. I doubt my memories. I'm sure it's a blessing. If I remembered those nights the way they actually unfolded, I'd be carrying a heap of embarrassment around with me.

*****

Erin had been living with us for almost three months when Mark's sister, Nicole, invited me to a "Girl's Night Out Birthday Party" at a bar called,

*On the Rocks*. Nicole and her friends—all moms—had taken to scheduling a night where they could get away and party their asses off. *On the Rock*s was an establishment in their rotation. It was located on Jasper Avenue in downtown Edmonton. Mark's younger cousin once told him that if he struck out at all other bars, he made his way there because it was a Cougar Bar, so he was sure to get laid. He was eighteen at the time, so anyone over thirty must have seemed like a Cougar to him.

I now had parenting in common with these women. But their relationships with their kids and husbands were different from what I was experiencing at home. They all married quite young and had their babies before the end of high school or in their early twenties. With this came many responsibilities: early mornings with crying newborns, breast feeding, and changing diapers. Of course, hangovers and sleeping in don't mix well with these tasks, so socializing late into the night often had consequences that made them avoid partying.

But now their children were older, and many of these women were recognizing that perhaps their high school sweetheart—whom they vowed to love forever—had turned into someone they didn't recognize anymore. Or had the men stayed who they were when they got married and the women changed? Some in the group were single for the first time. Some were bored with their partners. Some were still dedicated to their relationships, but excited to take a night off and be viewed as a sexy woman and not 'just a mom'. *They* were now the women wearing high heels and sultry smiles.

Now in my mid-thirties, I thought maybe I would fit in at the so-called Cougar Bar. My problem was that I had enough of the bar scene, but I liked Nicole and her friends and always had fun with them. I had only been parenting for a few months, but I needed a night out. I was excited to go just about anywhere, so I agreed. I told Mark I was going out with the Party Moms. He didn't love the idea of me hanging out at a nightclub, but he saw that I needed a break and told me to have a good time.

One of Nicole's friends—who was recently single—had booked a hotel room nearby for everyone to meet up beforehand. We'd have a couple of drinks while everyone got dolled up. It didn't take me long to get ready so I sat on the couch with my glass of red wine and watched the women. It was a well-rehearsed scene. Top 40 music played as the women conducted a small fashion show: at times making suggestions for a more flattering outfit or different jewelry, until a confirmed approval of "Cuuuute!" was declared by all.

Next, they used their well-worn hot irons to create seductive curls in their long hair. It was like a dance: hairspray was passed back and forth. As they primped in the mirror, hips swaying, they didn't miss a beat as they sang along to the music. I could see the transition in their eyes. With their motors revving, they morphed from "Mom" to "MILF."

Lipstick and perfume completed the ensemble. With one last sip of their wine, the Party Moms slipped into their heels, and like sexy little sports cars, they took off one by one out of the hotel door. Va-va-voom.

The bar was already busy when we arrived, but we managed to slink into the last booth off in the corner near the dance floor.

After we had settled, the first round of shooters arrived. Jägerbombs. I had never enjoyed shooters so, I had ordered a boring glass of wine. It stood out on the waitress's tray, tame in contrast to the Party Mom's daredevil drinks. After tapping their tiny shot glasses together for a cheers, they dropped the Jäger into the larger glass of Red Bull. The Party Moms threw their heads back and sent the bombs down their throats. They all let out an encouraging howl followed by a quick clap of their hands: the way football players break the huddle before getting back in the game to dominate their opponents.

"Let's go dance!" Nicole shouted to all the moms. It felt like the voltage of the entire bar had been turned up. The green and pink laser lights moved in a blur and the guitar player's deep vibratos slid through my eardrums.

I leaned into them, "I'll stay here," I nodded as I waved them off to go have fun.

They protested and pulled at my arms until I explained that it was a good idea for me to watch the purses. They stopped and appeared very logical for a moment; after all, they were still moms and it made sense to have someone watch the purses.

I slouched back into the padded booth. The Party Moms sauntered towards the dance floor, eager to shake what was locked and loaded in their tight dresses.

Throughout the night, I watched as they sashayed around the bar. They stood still to check their phones or text someone every so often. They snapped flirtatious selfies for their Facebook updates. I watched one of the women giggle and twirl the ends of her hair while standing shoulder to shoulder beside a well-dressed man who ordered them drinks from the busy bartender. I was happy to stay seated under the dim light and listen to the music. I didn't want to engage in conversation with any men. This didn't seem like a place that one could make small talk without someone getting the wrong idea. And I was certain that nobody was interested in hearing about my top priority: the Girl Guide cookies I needed to sell that week.

I kept my glass of Cab Sav up to my mouth most of the night. I had not worn lipstick, but I sensed a familiar purple stain from the wine permeating my lips. I peered over the rim. Taking small sips, like an intravenous drip, the alcohol saturated my bloodstream. Even though I felt out of place, I was relaxed. I realized in that bar that I wanted to be invisible and the Party Moms wanted to be seen. I didn't mind. I felt like I was watching a movie.

After leaving the bar, we all jumped into taxis and headed back to the hotel room. Once there, I could see that the evening of entertainment was not going to come to an end soon. Although I had planned on staying the night with the Party Moms, I ended up calling Mark to pick me up and bring me home.

I brushed my teeth, washed the make-up off my face, and crawled into bed. Shortly afterwards, I felt Erin poke my arm. "Get in." I whispered.

After that night, I declined so many more invitations from the Party Moms that they stopped inviting me out with time. Or maybe I was such a downer that they were happy I didn't go. Whatever the reason, I didn't take it personally. I figured at this point in their life, they wanted to drive in the fast lane with the top down, while I was happy to do the speed limit in a reliable Honda.

# SNAPSHOTS

Erin: "Maddie, what's a bikini line?"

Me: "It's the area right near your vulva where the bottom of your bikini sits. A lot of women will shave their bikini line so that hair doesn't show when they're wearing a bikini.

Erin: "Your hair—down there—can grow all the way... over there?"

Me: "Well, pubic hair generally grows in a triangle shape. So yeah."

Erin: "Like a beard?!"

Me: "Sort of I guess."

Erin: "Oh my God!"

# Chapter 6

# CURTIS AND JAMES

We made it to June without getting evicted and bought a house. While packing up for our move that would take place in early July, Mark got a call from Foster Care in British Columbia. They had removed the boys from his ex-wife's home. Mark called a lawyer. It took almost two weeks, but through a court process Mark fought and got an *ex parte* order, which meant that the boys could be released to him. He had to fly to the Island to pick them up immediately. He was on a flight within three hours of getting the call.

In the years prior to this, we had dealt with so many branches of family law that we had almost lost hope that anyone would help us. I remember watching an Amber alert. As we listened to the details of the missing child, Mark said, "I wonder if it's a dad taking his kid because the other parent is horrible and he can't get the courts to grant him custody."

For so many years, Mark flew out to visit the kids as often as possible. We also brought Curtis and Erin out to visit us in Alberta a couple of times. With only two to three weeks holidays in a year, and some long weekends, Mark did the best he could. Even though he called them a few times a week, it was a struggle to keep a strong connection.

Over the last few years that the children lived with their biological mother, Mark received emails and phone calls from random strangers who knew her. They begged him to come and take the kids. They told Mark that the boys had atrocious personal hygiene, that sometimes they were found wandering around alone where they shouldn't be, and that they didn't go to school. Realizing his children were being neglected, Mark pleaded with these people to report their observations to Child and Family Services. He explained that he could not go in and 'take' them. Some said they would call. They did, but we didn't know about it at that time because nothing changed. Mark often called their schools (which often changed) asking for copies of their report cards, but they didn't call him back. When we finally received their school documents, which were heartbreaking, his ex-wife had Mark listed as "estranged".

After so many injustices over those years, it had come to a breaking point that worked in our favour. Mark landed on the Island. That evening I received a text: "I have the boys."

The next day they flew back. I arrived home from work a few hours after Mark had settled in with them. Curtis jumped out from behind a wall to scare me as I entered. I gave him a hug and we both laughed. I was relieved to see him smiling and looking happy to be here with us. James sat in front of the TV and when I asked him how he was, he tilted his head towards me but kept his eyes locked on the cartoon he was watching. I asked again and this time he glanced over and nodded before returning his gaze to the screen. This didn't seem unusual to me. James was a kid of few words and even when he did speak, he sounded like a toddler. I could barely understand him.

Mark and I slipped off to the bedroom to talk. He told me he felt like he was kidnapping them. Any of the authorities he spoke with told him to return to Alberta as soon as possible before she found out and tried to stop him.

That night I made fried chicken, Caesar salad, and garlic toast for dinner. Curtis and James only wanted to eat the toast. I asked Erin to help me serve the food. I watched her hesitate as she offered the plate of food to Curtis, as though she could predict what was about to unfold. He picked the largest slice of garlic toast from the dish. I saw her chin twitch and, in that moment, it was as if a new child inhabited her body. Exclaiming, baby-like, she said, "I wanted that one!" Her eyes tightened and tears flowed out.

Erin had been with us almost six months by then. As the only child living with us, she hadn't had to share anything. In fact, we spoiled her quite a bit. I didn't think the situation matched the emotional breakdown and I was stunned. It was as though her whole world came crashing down. And in a way, it did. A new world would be re-built with the boys back in it, and it would be different from the last six months.

Curtis remained nonchalant the entire time and took a big bite of his toast. Crumbs jumped everywhere. "This is how she always is," he said.

We still had to remain in the apartment for another week and a half, but now our landlords were showing prospective tenants the place. The five of us turned our apartment into a tornado of cardboard boxes. All three kids were sitting there while people viewed our one bedroom home. The jig was up. We didn't say anything to the owners and—thankfully—the owners didn't say anything to us.

James was now seven and Curtis was ten. All three were still small enough to share the air mattress, which had developed a small leak. I woke up every morning to see the plastic bed half deflated underneath their little bodies: Erin always hanging half on the ground, James nestled between the wall and the mattress, and Curtis somewhere in the middle. It looked so uncomfortable. But they insisted on sleeping on it together. Erin didn't wake me up at all those nights.

I knew that once out of the apartment, we would begin building our new world. There were still court dates and drama to come, but we didn't care at the time. All that mattered was that we had all three kids with us. I could not wait to move out and get started in our new home. Putting this chapter behind us couldn't come soon enough.

# Chapter 7

# SUMMER

The house we bought was located in a cul-de-sac surrounded by other young families. The day we unloaded our U-Haul, Mark ordered pizza for everyone. Curtis and Erin joined in, but James ran out of the room screaming and crying. He didn't like pizza. He didn't like much when it came to food.

The boys came to us with a host of unique problems. They had developed encopresis; this is a condition described as chronic constipation caused by emotional or psychiatric disturbances. They lacked control of their bowels and soiled themselves several times a day, without feeling it. This wasn't a new problem; we had to contend with it during our visits with them on the Island as well, so it wasn't a surprise to see it continue.

It was a problem that the boys didn't know how to solve on their own and didn't seem to care about solving at all, as mystifying as that sounds. When it was obvious to our noses that an accident had happened, they lied about it. Mark had to bring the boys into the bathroom and let them see that he knew and go through the stages of a clean-up. They claimed they could not tell when to go to the bathroom, so we begged them to at least tell us when it occurred so that we could help guide them to learn. But they continued, straight faced, denying there was a problem. We kept finding dirty underwear hidden everywhere.

We tried for several surreal weeks to prompt them to admit this was an issue and to accept that we wanted to help them. We resorted to putting Pull-Ups on James. Curtis flat out refused. Mark began losing his tolerance with their dismissal of the situation and a lot of shouting began coming through the bathroom walls. It was the constant denial and secrecy that we could not bear. We took them to a psychologist and a doctor—who suggested stool softeners. This didn't cure the problem.

They were on summer break, so we were happy that we had time to address the issue before sending them to a new school. But with Mark and myself working, we had to leave them with Nicole and her husband, Uncle B, during the weekdays. Thank God they helped us. I don't know what we would have done without them. But with four kids of their own, they didn't have time to monitor the boy's bathroom schedule. With no end in sight, and all of our prevention methods failing, all we could do was try to control it as best we could.

Changing their diets was my main strategy. They ate little other than cereal, chicken nuggets, or peanut butter sandwiches. I knew as a nutritionist that these foods weren't helping their digestive systems function properly. They needed more fibre, water, and nutrients. I coached clients on how to eat better but felt like a huge failure in my own home.

It was a painful process. There were times the boys stared at their food while Mark sat with them, not speaking. Sometimes it was minutes, sometimes it was hours. With Mark's patience and sometimes non-negotiable dad voice, they tried new foods. He made them finish, or at least take a few bites of their meals. There were only so many hours in a day. It was a continuing battle of wills. We tried kid-friendly Kraft Dinner as a transition food, but even that resulted in a torrent of tears from James. Mark had to sit and watch him eat one noodle at a time, with a sip of milk after every bite.

I spent a great deal of time making healthy meals, trying all sorts of recipes. Erin had a decent appetite and ate most of the food I served, but the boys asked for McDonald's all the time. Fucking McDonald's. I was a nutritionist, for God's sake. It was infuriating. Maybe I was impatient and my expectations too high. I would have given a trophy to anyone who could get the boys to eat a green vegetable.

I decided to get them involved in planning meals. I sat with them on the couch and we searched the net. They didn't seem interested in much, that is, until Curtis saw a wrap recipe. The original recipe had sandwich meat, cheese, Ranch and mayonnaise dressing. The boys wanted to eat this every night, and they did for weeks. They insisted I write the "recipe" onto one of my recipe cards so that I didn't forget how to make it. We made that wrap so often that it is burned in my brain forever. It evolved and I discovered a way to add in lettuce. Somehow this simple Tortilla wrap changed our lives. I had no idea how many variations we could make. We moved on to Chicken Caesar salad wraps, tuna wraps, and beef taco wraps. I *finally* found a segue into healthier meals.

# Chapter 8

# RED RASPBERRIES

One of my fondest family memories as a child was foraging for berries. My parents divorced when I was ten, but before that they took my brother, two sisters, and me out to the country to pick wild blueberries.

"Watch for bears. Make some noise while you're walking." They warned us. "Check that you can always see the car so you don't get lost." It was the 80's, but my dad drove an old '62 faded grey Chevy Belair. He parked it on a back road, and we ventured into the tall trees to search for blueberry bushes.

Veering off in my own direction, I walked around, scanning for berries. After a few minutes in, I looked up to see my mom in the distance picking away at a blueberry patch and filling her pail while popping some ripe berries into her mouth. Inspired, I continued my search. I always stuck pretty close to my sister, Jennifer. She was only three years older than me, so we spent most of our time together. One of us shouted out when we came upon a patch: "Over here!" We never experienced any joy in hoarding the berries—though I did take pride in discovering a patch before her—but the excitement came when we shared our bounty.

Back then, blueberries found deep in the Manitoba forests were a treasure, although our own yard at home on our acreage held an abundance of trees and bushes we harvested from. We lived outside a small town in a little house that my dad and grandpa built. The house was made to be small and simple on purpose; my dad crafted us an old-fashioned lifestyle which helped him preach his minimalist values. He was determined to show us what this kind of living could teach: less is more. The real gem was our big backyard that we filled with adventure. Growing and harvesting from a garden on our property was part of the fun.

We also had an array of untamed options. A chokecherry tree with its deep purple and red-hued berries gave us an astringent treat; a rose bush with pink petals to pluck and rest delicately on our tongues was my favourite to show off to visitors. "You can eat these." I urged my skeptical friends to join in. Raspberry bushes flourished at the back of the property. I never took the sweet and sour taste of those red berries for granted.

In the springtime, dandelions shot up everywhere and we chewed on the young leaves before they turned bitter. I gathered the bright yellow dandelion flowers and arranged them beside the light pink clover blossoms that grew down by a short bridge. I gave the bouquet to my mom with a little note that read, "I love you."

Most years, my mom planted a modest garden, but many of our neighbours had beautiful larger plots. Jennifer and I snuck over to dig out a couple of veggies. Brushing off the soil, we'd chomp down on bright orange carrots as we snuck them back to our yard, acting like we got away with stealing gold. Bachelor Brian, from across the road, grew rows of rich green peas. We always appreciated his invitation to come pick a pail. To this day I can't eat a fresh pea without flashbacks of sitting in his garden watching the setting sun.

We spent many years visiting strawberry farms and paying a small sum to pick to our heart's content. We ate them straight out of the pail during the car ride back. My mom waited until we arrived home. Once in our kitchen I watched her wash and cut the strawberries, then place them in a small bowl. She seemed to enjoy the process. She poured fresh cream over them and a sprinkle of sugar: her favourite sweet treat.

When the fall harvest was ready, sweet corn was abundant. If we had not grown our own that year, we bought it from a guy parked on the side of the highway selling bags out of the back of his pick-up truck. After pulling the husk and silk away, we boiled the bright yellow corn and slathered it in butter with a sprinkle of salt. My mom threw down a large blanket in the backyard where we sat and ate the corn while welcoming the dusky sky. The massive mosquito population, which Manitoba was, and is still known for, would have declined by this time of year. Sitting outside while twilight tiptoed in was special indeed.

I wanted to infuse an appreciation for these simple parts of childhood into the kids' lives. After too many beautiful summer days wasted with them sitting downstairs playing video games, I could not stand the thought of it anymore. On my day off work, I was going to treat them to a glimpse of my childhood and the raw joy one could get from nature's bounty. They didn't know what they were missing. I was raising these kids now and they were going to get this gift from me. They just needed the guidance.

I decided we'd set off on a field trip. I told them we'd have fresh raspberries for dessert that evening, but that we wouldn't be paying the inflated price of $6.00 for a tiny container the size of a handful from the store. Instead, we would venture to a spot I knew of down near Miquelon Lake and pick our own berries for free.

The year before, I hiked the four-kilometre Grouse Loop at the Lake by myself. I picked that trail because it was longer and fewer people chose it. The peaceful environment felt like a sanctuary. An added bonus came in the last kilometre, when I discovered many raspberry bushes and spent an additional half an hour meandering along the trail plucking and gobbling up these juicy berries in pure bliss.

Miquelon Lake was over an hour-long drive from our home. The kids climbed into the car and we started off. I decided that no matter what, I was going to keep the excitement up so that they could enjoy themselves. I asked them if they ever picked their own berries and they told me that they had not. "Well, you guys are in for a treat!"

Ten minutes into the ride Erin asked if we were there yet. Her impatience hit a nerve and I snapped back, "No. We still have almost an hour of driving!"

I pointed out the fields of horses and cows on the periphery of the highway. I knew they had a thing for watching the animals and it seemed to pacify them as I drove on.

Once we arrived, we parked in an old field that led to the start of many trails. It had slipped my mind that the trails didn't begin until you walked about a kilometre into the wooded area. This wasn't a significant jaunt to me, but I had never hiked with the children in any lengthy fashion and had not considered that it was going to indeed be significant to them. Curtis and Erin complained about the long walk almost immediately. I kept reassuring them that it wasn't much farther and we'd come all this way to get the best berries they had ever seen. James was somehow on board with this pursuit so the two of us banded together to keep everyone's spirits up.

Finally, we reached the marked entrance to the Grouse Loop. Instead of starting off at the beginning of the loop, we began at the end where I knew we'd get to the berries quickest. That was when Erin panicked. She had spotted a bee and began running around in small circles. As we stood still, she used our bodies as pillars to swing herself around and out of the bee's jumpy swoops. Her gasps turned into small shrieks. "Erin. Stop running around. He's going to keep chasing you," I said. I kept walking and signalled the kids to follow me.

They walked behind me asking where the berries were. Once again, I had forgotten that they were about a half kilometre down this trail. Ugh! I didn't know how long I could keep them on this journey with me. Somehow, James was still excited about the prospect of eating handfuls of fresh raspberries. His palate was expanding, and I wanted to take this as an opportunity to show him how much fun it could be to pick delicious fruit. I could not believe my bad luck when another bee decided to fly alongside us as we walked. Curtis and Erin discovered it first and now both of them began the familiar shrieking bee dance. I tried to move on without paying much attention to this, still encouraging them to ignore the bee. To their credit, they did their best and the bee buzzed off.

Finally, I spotted our first red raspberry. I pointed it out to the kids, "Look there." Together we walked over to the bush, where I plucked off the berry and asked with enthusiasm who wanted to eat it. Curtis and Erin didn't look at all interested. This disappointed me but I didn't show it. James's face lit up, "I will!" I gave it to him, and he popped it in his mouth. I was so thankful for James.

I wasn't going to give up. The berries weren't as abundant as the previous year but we ran into more and more along the way.

"Bingo!" I called out when I discovered a good patch. Soon James was imitating me: "Bingo! Bingo!" Curtis and Erin walked along beside us. They pointed out a few berries here and there and even made a small effort to pick a few but I could tell they were more concerned with spotting menacing bees than berries. I didn't care much at this point as James and I were enjoying ourselves and getting more and more excited about the ever-growing bounty in our Tupperware container.

Once we had a good amount, we started back, continuing to keep our eyes out for any that we missed. James and I laughed and threw berries in our mouths while discussing how impressed Dad was going to be with the dessert tonight. The other two walked ahead of us, focused on getting to the exit. I could hear them grumbling to one another but didn't pay much attention to their disenchantment. James and I stopped often and yelled, "Bingo!" They stood there tapping their feet, waiting for us. We ignored them as we picked more berries.

Then I heard Erin's scream. "Bee!" I looked up from the patch James and I were working on to see Curtis and Erin running, screaming, arms flailing. The trail veered off and they disappeared. James and I looked at each other.

"I guess we should go find them."

He shrugged. "Yeah, I guess so."

We weren't far from the end of the loop, but I was worried that in their frenzy they would get lost. Once we got to the exit sign, they were both standing there unimpressed.

"You guys okay?"

Erin stuck her hands on her hips and wide-eyed declared, "Well we were getting chased by bees."

"I know. All right, let's go then," I was happy to leave at this point, too.

We made our way back to the car and rolled down the windows. Back on the highway, I was glad to be heading home. This was enough excitement—and disappointment—for one day. Just when I thought our adventure was over, Erin screamed.

"What's wrong?" I yelled out.

"There's a bee back here. It's on James's hand!" Now it was James's turn to scream.

I was doing 110 kilometres an hour and had to stop as fast as possible on the gravel shoulder without causing an accident. I jumped out of the car, flung open the rear door, and swatted the bee away from James's hand. The dust around me settled and I saw that the bee was dead. James had a jacket over his head and was sitting so still he seemed paralyzed.

"Why is there a jacket on his head?" I asked.

"I threw it there so that he didn't see the bee." Erin looked at me like that should have been obvious.

I backed out of the car and took a deep breath. I reached in and pulled the jacket off of James's head. He had tears in his eyes. It broke my heart.

"Wanna go to McDonald's?" I asked.

James nodded. "Yays" came from the other two. I got back into the driver's seat, feeling as far from the driver's seat as possible.

After some ice cream cones at shitty McDonald's, we arrived home. I put ointment on James's sting and sent them downstairs to watch TV before plopping down on the couch to stare at nothing.

When Mark arrived home from work, we stood in the kitchen while I told him about our adventure. By this time, I could almost laugh about it, but I was still baffled. "You know, some of my best memories are picking wild blueberries in the forest with my family. I thought the kids would feel the same."

"They want to play video games," Mark said. The truth hurt.

"Had *I* raised them, they would have different values." I shifted gears, "Anyway, look at all the raspberries we got. Eat some!"

Mark reached for a handful and popped them into his mouth. He nodded at me and took some more. Then he stopped chewing and spit the raspberries into the garbage.

"What's wrong?"

"Worms."

I walked over and examined the container. Sure enough, teeny tiny little worms crawled all over our wild berries.

"Are you kidding me?" I took another deep breath. "I'm going to lie down." I walked off to the bedroom.

"I'm going to lie down" was a sentence I came to use more and more often. I realized that these three children may never value what I value, and that I might never truly bond the way I wanted to bond with them. I needed to close my eyes for a little while, before I could reset and take on the next adventure (or disaster) of stepparenting.

# Chapter 9

# FAIRMONT

Biker Nana planned another annual trip. Mark, the kids, and I, along with Nicole's family, agreed to join her in Fairmont, B.C. We would all meet up there and stay a few days in a mountain resort. In total, there were five adults and seven children.

I found that living as a prairie girl for so many years didn't prepare me for spending time in the mountains. The mountains are everything people say they are; overused adjectives like 'majestic' and 'stunning' are in everyone's re-telling of their journeys throughout Alberta and British Columbia. I had developed a taste for hiking in them on our couples' getaways. But when I've surrounded myself with the jagged mountains for more than a week or so, the brisk air and serenity of it all transforms into something else. An internal switch somewhere deep inside me flips. My chest tightens. I feel constricted, and small. In the evening, the multiple mountain peaks and their colourless grey broken edges pull the bright warming sun from view too early. The timing is off, unpredictable. I miss a step.

From there, a darkness descends, and loneliness takes hold of me. If clouds roll in, I feel a shiver that penetrates my bones, and creates a bitter emotional chill. It isn't lost on me that many of my former visits spent in the mountains have been during unsettling and even heartbreaking times. Whether this is the reason for these unfortunate symptoms or not, I don't know. I suspect a connection.

The more I discover the world around me, the more I'm certain that the prairies live in my heart. Driving down a gravel road in between tall wheat fields swaying in the warm breeze helps me breathe. And although watching the sun descend below a distant pink sky can sometimes make me feel lonesome, more often, it makes me feel grounded.

But these were the mountains, the full-on Rockies that we were driving through on our family vacation to Fairmont. It was an eight-hour drive, which isn't so bad, but this was not a ride I could tolerate in any sober state. Swooping in and out of tunnels and then swerving through segments of sharp-walled rocks on one side and dooming cliffs on the other made me feel like a china dish in a cabinet during a looming tornado. In my usual manner, I packed a to-go coffee cup of wine to sip on while Mark drove. Illegal? Yes. Worth the charge if caught? Hell, yeah. I rolled the dice on this one. If I stayed around thirty percent intoxicated on these rides, the alcohol coated my frayed nerves and the adrenaline twitch subsided. Otherwise I transformed into a lunatic-backseat-driver, pumping imaginary brakes on the passenger side while pointing at perceived dangers mumbling, "Watch out!…Okay, never mind. I thought we were a little too close there. Phew! ….Whoa! Maybe we are a little too close! No, no, we're fine…."

Mark glanced sideways at me. He dug deep to stay patient with me and probably loved me a little less when we took these kinds of road trips. He would never admit that, but even *I* loved me a little less when we travelled through the mountains.

I envied anyone who could enjoy this scenery; but it wasn't only this car ride that bothered me, I was having trouble relaxing at the best of times this summer. A complicated chapter in our lives had opened up when we got the kids and it wasn't ending any time soon

Eventually we made it to Fairmont Hot Springs. A family of deer rested in a neighbourhood front yard as we drove by. The mountains were a little off in the distance, giving me some space. We found our resort and I exhaled as we unloaded our bags.

Nicole's family arrived a few hours later. Mark and I were outside when Biker Nana pulled up on her motorcycle, her hair flying beneath her helmet in the wind. Cheryl was around five foot seven and weighed 120 pounds. She was so light that she couldn't push her Harley down far enough for her to touch the ground. She had to wear biker boots with a two-inch heel to reach the road. She had been on the highway straddling her Electra Glide for over two days, alone, from Vancouver Island to meet us here.

I gave her a hug. "How was driving the bike for that many hours?"

She pulled back, "*Drive?* You don't *drive* motorcycles. You ride them!"

I threw my hands in the air as though I was giving up. "Well what the hell do I know about motorcycles?"

She rolled her eyes, "Clearly nothing."

We both laughed.

Once everyone was settled in, we planned our agenda for the week. The children and their cousins all talked at once while reading off the family-geared events on the calendar. There were contests, scavenger hunts, and swimming for the whole family and some evening activities for the adults. It reminded me of the resort in the movie *Dirty Dancing*, without the dirty dancing.

I gave a little shriek and clapped my hands when I saw that I could sign up for hikes all week. This was going to be the highlight of the trip for me. I'd go along with the kid stuff of course, but knowing that I would wake up to a hike was going to be the "me time" on this trip that I so badly needed.

I was also looking forward to spending quality time with the kids. Our raspberry picking adventure had been a failure, but I still had hope that they would connect with nature. We had been cooped up in our house all summer, unpacking and getting accustomed to one another. Now was the time for us to find some rugged trails, pick some juniper berries, and wander next to wildlife. What a great opportunity. I'd try to make it more interesting this time and Mark would be there, so he'd help guide me to make it a success.

The next day, we planned a picnic. Mark and I made sandwiches and headed off with Curtis, Erin, and James, to an open area off a trail with large trees and a stream running through it. We sat down and pulled out our sandwiches. I had taken only two bites from my peanut butter and jam when I saw the wasp. It was like a bad joke. Anytime I hoped to explore nature with the kids, some flying shithead with a stinger showed up and ruined everything. Erin stood up but didn't move this time. Curtis threw his sandwich down, jumped up, punched the air, and ran off screaming. I shrugged my shoulders and took a picture of him running. I thought it could be funny one day. One day. James handled it well considering he was the actual victim last time. He stood up but kept eating his food like nothing was happening. We were all standing now, waiting a minute for Curtis to return. The moment lost any magic I was hoping to find so I suggested Mark look for him while I pack up the food. I felt defeated once again but tried to shake it off. It was over even before it started.

A few days passed. Kids yelled and chased each other. Doors flung open between rooms. The encopresis was an issue, especially when considering pools and hot tubs. Something didn't feel right. The noise. The loud unpredictable sounds jolted my adrenal glands. I felt caged in a crazy zoo and saw no escape. I started to feel my mind unravel. Everyone else seemed so normal. When the family went off to another event, I told Mark I needed some time and locked the hotel door behind him.

I sobbed. I felt out of place and helpless. I was emotionally suffocating. I was now the mom of three kids I didn't understand. Everything was so fucked up. I kept returning to the same thoughts; they would be different if I had been their biological mother. I'd feel closer to them. They would understand and share my values.

But that was never going to be a reality. This dialogue I had with myself was a broken record playing over in my head. They were here, and they were the way they were, and I was the way I was. We were all a heaping mess of chaos and it didn't seem to bother anyone else the way it bothered me. I could not acclimatize quickly enough. *Maybe I never would.*

After half an hour, I got off the couch and glanced at myself in the bathroom mirror. I saw a woman who was defeated. I felt ashamed that I wasn't stronger. My eyes were glossy. As much as I tried to stop crying, the tears kept welling up. My eyelids would swell and everyone would see behind the mask if I didn't stop.

Mark came back to the room to check on me. I was still a mess. Through my weeping I gasped to catch my breath and repeated, "I don't know how to do this. I feel like I'm going crazy." I remember the fear and sadness on his face. He didn't say anything, but I sensed he wanted to understand me.

I couldn't sit there and cry forever. I hoped that deep down I was tougher than that. I put on a pair of sunglasses and went for a hike alone, to ground myself.

Hiking up the side of the grassy hill gave me just what I needed: solitude and a scenic view that looked like a slice of heaven. Juniper shrubs lined the trail leading to the top. I made a mental note to come back with a container and pick some of the purple berries to bring back to Edmonton with me. Although I knew that juniper berries were used to make gin, I had learned of a way to use them in an herbal recipe to help the body detox.

I continued up hill and found myself entering a forested area. Small streams of sunbeams filtered through the branches on the tall trees, illuminating the terrain. I stopped to close my eyes and take a deep breath to connect with the earthy scents of the damp soil, the leaves on the plants, the herbs, and the bark on the trees. I listened to the quiet, and the light breeze shuffling a few leaves above my head. A bird sang out. I felt a shift in my body, my shoulders relaxed and the heaviness lifted from me. I was calm. I was reminded that *this* is who I am. At least, this is who I wanted to be.

After I had rejected religion as a teen, and experienced so much anxiety, I came to realize something pivotal: my walks in nature were a place that offered me a profound peace of mind and helped me connect to the earth and to myself.

I felt gratitude being in the wilderness, the rawness reminding me that life doesn't need to be so complicated. There have been times I've looked out at the land from high up on a rocky mountain, or on the prairies across a yellow flowered field, and teared up over the beauty and wholeness in my soul that I experience. During my walks I've found myself praying to a creator, to a God. I imagine, and hope, that many religious people feel this way when worshipping in their church or temple. I've never been able to nail down what my spiritual beliefs should be called, although, I don't feel a need to put a name to it. I've found what works for me.

As I continued walking, an old-world medicine herb called Usnea, or what's commonly known as "Old Man's Beard" hung down from the trees. True to this lichen's name, the greyish green colour and texture does resemble an old man's beard. I admired the abundance of this herbal remedy that helps with the immune system and began thinking about how much I valued herbal medicine and its power. It was a strong value of mine, one that neither the kids nor Mark shared.

Towards the end of my hike, I happened upon an older gentleman. We started talking and he shared that he was a retired teacher. He asked where my family was, and I explained that my kids weren't much for hiking. I even complained a little about video games and told him that's all they seemed to want to do; that they didn't share my values and that it bothered me. He told me that air-conditioning ruined it for everyone. I asked him what he meant. He explained that before air-conditioning, people used to go outside because their houses got so hot inside. Families sat on their porches, fanning away the hot beads of sweat while talking to their neighbours who were doing the same thing, getting to know them, maybe becoming friends. Children played outside more, rode bikes, got in fights, and figured out how to solve them. Today we all stayed inside and not many homes had porches anymore. I enjoyed his company and the short conversation, telling him so before moving forward on my own.

His words stayed in my head. It was a cultural change that affected plenty of homes, not only mine. A sad reality crept in. Was I living in the wrong era?

I walked a little more. It was an hour or so since I had left Mark in the room.

Something shifted while I walked back into the resort. I felt renewed, determined to try again. I was back, Baby! I also may have been a little drunk as I had brought my wine filled coffee cup on the hike.

Mark and the kids were making lunch when I walked in. I scanned the room for sheets of paper and found a few. I snatched them up, sat down beside Erin, and said, "Wanna make a canoe out of this paper?"

When we were children, Jennifer and I made paper canoes and tried to float them through the small culvert beneath our driveway. This was an open ended metal pipe that water streamed through to flow from one ditch to the next. Every spring after the snow had melted and the rain came, we created a pile of paper canoes and tried to sail them in the ditches and puddles of water around our home. Sometimes we even put my brother's green plastic army men in them. Splashing around in our rubber boots, we spent all weekend racing the paper boats.

Erin and I made up a bunch of canoes. The boys weren't paying much attention until I said, "We're going to sail these boats outside through the culverts. Are you guys in?" Surprisingly, they jumped up and put on their sandals. Mark looked up at me as he continued prepping lunch. "You okay? Where are you going?"

I opened the door while they ran out. "We'll be back in an hour." I was on a mission.

A short distance away we found a couple of large culverts with clean water flowing through them. We all climbed down the large rocks to get near the shallow water. We raced our boats. Some flopped right away. But they got the hang of the current and where they could set them in the water. I felt like a kid again. I sat down on the big grey concrete culvert. James sat in front of me and we watched the other two race their canoes.

He looked up at me with his bright blue eyes and the sweetest smile and said, "I love you."

"I love you too, James."

It wasn't such a bad day after all.

## SNAPSHOTS

*James on my lap playing with my arms*

"You have really flabby arms!"

Me: "Oh yeah? Thanks a lot. Dad has all the muscle, I guess."

James: "Yep! He's strong and you're loooooong!"

Me: "I guess so."

James: "You know, maybe you can stretch the skin and fly!"

Me: "All right. Take a hike, kid."

# Chapter 10

# MOM BRAIN

Even with the canoe success of our holiday trip, the overall summer had been a disaster for me. Thank God it was almost over. I had committed to a situation that felt out of control. This was my favourite season, but even the sun with its warmth couldn't rouse me out of bed on a Saturday morning.

Saturdays used to hold a mystery for me: a mystery that unfolded as the day progressed. Where would I find myself? Who would I see? For years I relished this spontaneity. Awaking on a Saturday morning—without children—meant I had the luxury of designing the mystery while sipping my coffee. It took minutes to throw my hair up in a messy bun, slip into my flip flops, and walk out the door. It was so simple. Maybe I would stroll through the farmers' market taking my time smelling the ripe B.C. peaches. I'd move on to the next booth, thinking nothing about paying a little extra for locally grown produce. Or maybe the mystery would inspire me to steer my car to a park where I'd walk barefoot on a field of lush grass and sit for hours reading my book while enjoying the warm breeze on my face. A friendly little ant might run across my toes.

Now I awoke to a five hundred piece puzzle. Which pieces would the kids hand me today? What pieces did Mark and I hold? Could our pieces fit together? There were too many tasks to organize, too many lists to tend to, too many chores. I could not think with any clarity anymore. Was this what 'Mommy Brain' felt like? Had my cerebral cortex turned into mashed potatoes?

I wanted to take the kids out for a hike, but I didn't have any enthusiasm left to make it through their potential grumbles. The risk of having to deal with the encopresis in public was also a deterrent. I saw the radiant day from my bedroom window, and all too often I closed the blinds and turned away. I grieved my freedom.

Mark heard about it. Mark heard about it every day. My words, heavy like bricks, fell between us in arguments, creating a larger pile to climb over every time. I complained and I cried. Some days, Mark felt the same strain and cried with me. The repetitive and desperate exasperation kept tumbling out of my mouth. I knew it didn't help to point out all of the challenges. It was just making things worse for Mark. These arguments were damaging to us as a couple. But I couldn't help feeling like all I wanted to do was run away and hide out in a quiet cave, far from everyone in the world.

I decided to try and stay silent to keep the toxic words from him. Unspoken, they lodged in my throat. I held them. Invisible. I swallowed them so often that I could feel them corroding my heart. I resented the kids. I was becoming depressed for the first time in many, many years.

In the beginning, I placed it all logically in my head: we'd give them a good life because we were responsible, and we'd nourish them and teach them how to be kind human beings. We wouldn't fail at this. They would be successful in life because it could not be any other way. It was black and white to me. Linear. My anxiety always forced me to compartmentalize and try to control the situation. But this situation was anything but linear.

I was zig zagging all over the place. I had believed it was just a matter of having them around healthy and happy parents and they would "fall into place". Why did I think that? I *never* fooled myself into thinking it would be easy, but I had no idea that depression would begin to seep in. I couldn't make sense of what—to me—made no sense at all: child psychology.

Not only was I failing at Motherhood, I also didn't recognize myself. How did other moms cope? If I could talk to some trusted friends, maybe they could assure me that I wasn't losing my fucking mind. I made plans to visit Summer, Lina, and Robyne to get some advice.

## SUMMER

My good friend Summer had a daughter who was five years old. When I told her what I was feeling she said, "You know what I Googled the other day? 'Why don't I like my kid?'" She was wide eyed and nodding at me as she talked. "You're not the only one who's going nuts."

Years ago, when I first met Summer, she disclosed juicy details of wild nights from her trips to Mexico. She loved dancing, socializing, and was free-spirited. She travelled often and enjoyed different cultures. Now Summer was a responsible mom and a single parent. She never said it, but I felt she grieved the freedom of her former life as well.

I knew she loved her daughter. That was never in question. But now that I was a parent, I saw her situation better and understood her true frustration. She received no financial or emotional support from the father. The pregnancy had been a surprise. Once she realized that she could not count on anything from the birth father, she decided to raise her daughter on her own.

A few months after giving birth, I asked what she thought of parenthood. She grinned and said, "I don't recommend it." Most of the time she joked about her tough situation. She pretended to pull out her hair, crossed her eyes, and said, "It's crazy!" She was good at making light of the challenges. The years went by and she continued to work hard and support herself while trying to perform the relentless task of being almost *everything* to her daughter.

"I never get a minute to myself," she said in a matter-of-fact way.

We continued to complain with bursts of laughter sprinkled in. If we didn't see the humour in it, we'd have cried. Summer and I tried to be upbeat and positive, and even though we commiserated (and continued to for years) we always knew that the other had good advice worthy of sharing.

## LINA

Lina was one of the most interesting people I met when I moved to Edmonton. She was born in Alberta; both of her parents were Italian, and she was baptized Catholic. When she realized that the holy water sanctified by the priest didn't feel like anything but regular H2O, she became more of a philosopher in search. I met her through work a few years before she converted to Islam. Now a practicing Muslim, she embraced her religion the way she did most things in her life: with great intensity. She made the decision to cover her body and long dark brown hair in modesty, which made her a target of stereotyping.

Once we sat down at the cafe, Lina began our visit with a funny but sad story.

"I was pushing my daughter in her baby stroller and was having trouble getting it up over the curb, and this guy passes by me in his truck, rolls down his window, and yells, 'In Canada, we use sidewalks!'"

"Seriously? What an asshole," I said.

"I know. So, I yell back, "I was born here, you jerk!'" She shook her fist in the air and we erupted in laughter.

Lina adjusted her dark rimmed glasses and tucked bits of hair back under her pink hijab. I couldn't remember the last time I saw her uncovered. Her round face and big green eyes seemed more prominent now that her wavy dark locks were hidden from my view.

I was once talking with Lina when our co-worker suggested she pluck her full eyebrows. She replied that that wasn't always a thing in her religion.

She once told me, "Some people make assumptions about who I am now, and my background. I had a woman tell me that my English was great, and that she could not detect my accent. I also get some people asking me if my husband allows me to go to school."

We still worked together on and off, but Lina was focused on her Masters in History and Islamic studies. While pregnant with their daughter, she helped her husband open and run an elementary school in Morocco. She had moved back to Canada, bringing her Moroccan husband and daughter to live here for the first time while she pursued her studies.

In the past we used to attend Slam Poetry readings and Art events. Now we had less time and were lucky if we could find a couple of hours to catch up over lunch or coffee every few months. Whenever I asked her about her classes, projects, or latest travel, her advanced academia and philanthropy aroused passion in her voice. Her eyes kept contact with mine. Her words swirled around me, veiling me in a firestorm of inspiration, fury, and excitement. I loved it. It mesmerized me. During these times, she was fierce. It was hard to believe she was only five foot two.

She sat back and waited for me to speak. Sometimes I said, "I don't know what all of that means." Smiling sweetly without judgement, enough for me to see her snaggletooth, she explained it in layman's terms.

I would never beat Lina at a game of Trivial Pursuit, but we had enough in common; our humour was kindred and our love of writing kept us bonded. Not to mention, we both recently became mothers.

"You have some food in your scarf," I pointed.

She glanced down and found a little piece of her sandwich. "Seriously, I always get food in here. Legit Hijabi problems, am I right?"

"Do you care if I order a glass of wine?" I asked.

"No, I don't care, but I can't pay for it. It's not permissible."

Lina had invited me out for lunch.

"That's cool, I'll pay," I signalled for the waitress.

She protested that she wanted to treat me, but now I made it so that she could not. I imagined I did many things that were not permissible, like swearing, but Lina was kind enough to it slide. She never held others to the standards of her own faith.

I had seen Lina at a work meeting a few weeks back with her daughter in tow, but we had not visited alone in months so there was a lot to catch up on. I never had a problem being honest with her. I told her that I was losing my mind.

She understood right way. "There's so much stress on us to be perfect. Remember the last time we saw each other? When I realized I was pulling off bits of bread and feeding it to my daughter in a room full of nutritionists and herbalist, I thought that everyone was judging me for giving her gluten. You have to do your best and not worry about the rest," she said.

I worried so much it made me feel sick. "We finally got the boys to start eating other foods, but all they do is ask for McDonald's and Mac and Cheese. I spend all this time cooking wholesome meals and they want that junk. Can you believe it?" I asked.

She shrugged, "I ate Kraft Dinner when I was a kid."

"Yeah," I leaned back in my chair, "I did too. And I loved that shitty stuff." I paused. "But now that I know what's in it, I don't want to feed it to them. Have you read up on tartrazine? I don't want my kids to eat yellow number five! I even tried to imitate it and made a recipe from scratch. Of course, they didn't like it."

She shook her head in sympathy. "Sugar, gluten, trans fats, genetically modified foods, pesticides: they say everything is evil and the literature is always changing. Plus, who can afford organic stuff? What are we supposed to feed our children?"

She read my mind. Even as a nutritionist, it was a struggle.

"And we're supposed to work all day and come home and cook a nutritious meal? That takes *time*. Once you're finished, you have to do the dishes, get the kids to bathe, brush their teeth, read them a book, and put them to sleep. There's no time left in a day. We don't even have a TV on the main floor. I don't know how parents have time to watch TV."

I was on a roll: "Sometimes I stand when I eat now. I *stand* there in the kitchen wolfing down food, not even sitting and savouring it the way I used to. I hate that. It's like my little ceremonies throughout the day have disappeared. I can't even remember the last time I shaved my legs. I feel so confused."

She tilted her head. "There's too much pressure on parents. You're doing your best. You love the kids. That's all you can do."

## ROBYNE

I was on a flight to Winnipeg to visit family and my best friend Robyne. In the middle of the two hour flight, I remembered an animated conversation we had had a few years prior. It was the year we both turned twenty-nine:

"And then she said, 'What if you regret not having a baby?' Why do people say that?" I posed the rhetorical question as I shook my head and soured my face. I was in the middle of telling Robyne, about one of the ladies at work who was desperate to have a baby. When I told this co-worker I wasn't interested in having children, she couldn't believe it.

"Yeah," Robyne rolled her eyes. "I get that sometimes too. What did you tell her?" Robyne leaned in to hear me. The lounge where we were having dinner and drinks was noisy.

"I told her that I didn't think 'regret' was a good reason to get pregnant. I told her that I believe that you have to *want* a baby with every bone in your body and that I didn't possess this desire. It would be a fear-based decision. I don't think it's right to try to invent a feeling that isn't there."

"I get it," she said, "I think my parents believe my 'clock is ticking'".

I chimed in, "Oh yeah, I hear you. Get this: my mom, who always said, 'Don't have children if you don't want to', told me that I should freeze my eggs in case I change my mind."

We laughed, then raised our glasses to one another and took our last sip. Robyne motioned for the waitress to return so we could order more wine.

We were now in our mid-thirties. My flight landed and I called Robyne.

She wanted to have breakfast the next day.

As soon as we sat down, I could see something was on her mind. She seemed unusually quiet as we began to catch up. I was stunned when she announced that she and her husband were trying for a baby. It hadn't occurred to me that Robyne might change her mind. Our conversation about not having babies seemed so long ago. Because those conversations *were* so long ago. I had been with Mark for five years and a full-time stepmom for eight months at that point.

She explained that in the last few months she had gone through a miscarriage and she was now charting her ovulation. Sex on demand was becoming a chore for both her and her husband. The romance was getting sucked out of the relationship.

Robyne and her husband had fallen in love three years prior. Many nights were filled with fancy restaurants and bottles of wine. They gazed into one another's eyes and shared deep emotional secrets. Robyne, who had always maintained a slender figure, had gained an extra fifteen pounds and said she didn't care.

He proposed while on a cruise. Their pictures showed full smiles and happiness as they travelled the world, walking on sandy beaches and waking early to drink mimosas on a terrace in Italy.

Now Robyne looked tired. She was still optimistic, but unsure of the future. She didn't laugh at all.

I did the math and thought about how old she'd be when her child turned eighteen. Holy shit. Didn't she know that all of her freedom would be gone? Should I be the one to break it to her? Did she know she would never be able to throw on some flip flops, grab her sunglasses, and drive off to a café and sip a mochaccino? I watched her mouth moving but had stopped listening. I wanted to shake her and yell, "You won't be able to just… walk out of your house!"

I tuned back in to what she was saying. She seemed so sad. I could feel how much she wanted this. Who was I to tell her otherwise? So, in typical best friend fashion, I asked if there was anything I could do to help.

After all the fancy advice from doctors and many others in her life, Robyne decided to use cheap Dollar Store kits to figure out when she was ovulating. She said they worked as well as the expensive ones. Robyne was pregnant a few months later.

The conversations with these moms—my good friends—made me ponder. Even though I was feeling depressed, I wasn't alone. Their stories made me feel like I had someone who understood.

It was the end of August and every night I sat up late, planning how I could make our home happier for everyone. I opened a bottle of Merlot and poured myself a drink. What the hell did I know? I knew one thing for certain: We were all in the same boat together. If I was going to stay sane and keep this fucked-up boat afloat, it was going to take an ocean of wine.

## SNAPSHOTS

*Going through a grade two prep book, trying
to teach seven-year-old James to read*

As we sat there with the bright sunlight stretching through
the window, James looked up at me. His face jolted into
a surprised expression and he pointed at my face.

"Hey! You're growing a moustache!"

"What? Great, that's great, James."

He insisted, "No, you really are!"

"Whatever. Keep reading, kid."

# Chapter 11

# FLYING GALLEON

Back in Manitoba while we were still living in the country, I went to a French Immersion elementary school that had a playground with swings and monkey bars. Off to the side there was a piece of equipment that all the kids had a love/hate relationship with. It was called the merry-go-round. I have no idea how it got that name because the only thing it had in common with a proper amusement park merry-go-round—the kind that had hand-sculpted horses of vibrant colours—was that it spun in a circle. Unlike that kind of merry-go-round, this one didn't play any fancy music and there weren't any hopes and dreams attached to it. It was old and rickety and at one time had been painted a dark blue. The paint had faded and was chipped away from brutal Canadian winters, leaving this old heap of metal looking like it was ready for the junkyard.

It had a diameter of about nine feet across. The middle of the merry-go-round had a three-foot-tall solid steel pole and from there six steel spokes emerged evenly to the outside of the structure that children could hang on to. The steel beams were around waist high—if you were ten years old. It looked more like a medieval war machine than something students should play on.

Kids at my school didn't care. They took whatever they could get in those days to have fun. Living in this small town didn't allow for anything too special and many of us didn't know the difference.

The problem with this monstrosity was that it went fast. Dangerously fast. Students crammed onto it with no regard for safety. The bigger kids pushed the outside bars while running alongside; once it got going to what felt like warp speed, the older kids hopped back on the platform and everyone shrieked in dizzy delight. Inevitably, someone riding on the periphery of this machine went flying off, either taking out an unsuspecting bystander, or simply sailing through the air onto the hard ground. 'Whoa! There goes Duane!' Or some kid tripped while pushing the machine to go faster and got their leg sucked under. That accident was no joke. Every few months there was an announcement over the intercom that someone had gotten hurt on the merry-go-round and that the students were to stay away from it. You saw Johnny limping through the hallway for a week. Yet, slowly but surely, we were drawn back to the life threatening device. Teachers shrugged and turned a blind eye. I'm starting to think maybe they had their own thirty percent intoxication-inducing to-go coffee cup to get through managing recess.

When it rained, a deeply-grooved mud pit developed where the children were running to get it going. We got in trouble if we came back in from recess with dirty shoes, so we had to get creative with the push, leaning our bodies further away to keep our shoes half clean. Of course, this added a new element of wobbly danger.

I always preferred to ride with peers my age. They couldn't push it as fast as the older kids. I never had the stomach for anything that jerked my body around in a fast circle. So, when the big kids showed up, many of us younger ones bailed or learned the hard way. Most of the time the older students gave us fair warning that they intended to 'give'er'. Some of the smaller ones thought they could take it, but when that circle of death got going, at some point, you heard howls of "Stttopppp!" The bigger kids groaned as they slowed it down to let the frightened smaller students off. If I got stuck on there with a fast pusher, I crouched down and closed my eyes until the devastation was over. I wasn't going to be a howler.

During my teen years I lived in the city, where fairs passed through every year. Robyne and I went together. She was an adventure-seeker but I had flashbacks of stomach-churning merry-go-round fairies dancing in my head. As much as she begged me to get on the crazy spinning rides with her, I stepped back and pointed out the tamer ones I was willing to go on. These involved lower grade movement, and overall, she didn't give me too hard a time and humoured me by going on the lame rides. If she couldn't find anyone to venture on the big ones with her, she went alone. I stood back and waited by the carnie that had a pack of smokes snuggled in his white t-shirt sleeve, smiling and waving as I let cotton candy dissolve on my tongue.

One year, we went to the largest midway that passed through our city. It was The Red River Exhibition, but we all called it, "The Ex". I must have been feeling some unusual confidence on one trip because somehow, I was talked into going on a couple of rides that I otherwise would have met with a solid look of disdain. One was "The Boat". I never knew the official name of this ride, but this humongous boat rocked back and forth, higher and higher into the air. Nothing too over the top, and I remember having a lot of fun. This may have been the only time I remember feeling so carefree on an amusement ride.

Now I lived in Edmonton, home to one of the world's largest indoor amusement parks at West Edmonton Mall. Curtis' eleventh birthday was a few days away and he wanted to go. It was always crowded with kids and teens and the air smelled like lip gloss and farts, but I was willing to be a good sport. We loaded two cars with the children and their friends and headed off for an extravaganza of rides and cavity-causing treats.

Once we arrived, we split up, and I paired with James. I knew he just wanted to go on the little kid rides, and I would be sitting and waiting. Sure enough, James ran to line up at the kiddie rides where little tots screamed with glee and waved to their parents every time the miniature carousel went around. This was a real carousel and bore no resemblance to the decrepit merry-go-round of my childhood. Lights flashed and buttons buzzed when the children slapped the mechanics in the front of their race car or airplane. I stood watching, holding his jacket and wishing I had brought earplugs. I saw that other parents boarded the rides with their toddlers, sitting on the carousel platforms and stabilizing their kid. James took his place in the middle of it all, but I began re-thinking the ride he had chosen when I realized how much he stuck out like a huge bouncing buoy in a sea of four-year-olds. There he was, sitting on the kiddie convoy with a big goofy grin on his face, oblivious to his own size and age.

Once he was done, I pulled him aside and knelt down in front of him. "James, why don't you try a few of the bigger rides? You're not a toddler."

He hesitated, "But I like these rides."

"I know, but do you see how little these kids are?"

He glanced around. "Yeah."

"See how big you are? You just turned eight, right?"

He looked down at himself, "Yeah."

"Okay then, let's find something a little more exciting. I'll even go on with you."

He grinned, albeit with a little uncertainty.

Hand in hand, we walked around and observed the rides. Even though I didn't want to get on any rides, I felt it was important to expose James to something bigger and better. Then I saw the boat. *The Boat!* This was a sure thing. A large yellow and blue sign with painted stars hung above the ride: Flying Galleon. So that's what it was called. I looked up in awe. *Flying Galleon.* Memories of The Ex came rushing back as I remembered the excitement all those years ago.

"James!" I pointed, "Let's go on this. It'll be fun."

We stood in line watching the boat, the anticipation building. He watched the bigger kids and young teens waving their arms in the air and laughing as the boat sailed back and forth. "Do you see how much fun they're having?" I said. He squirmed his mouth to one side, unsure, but said he would try it. I was proud of him for taking a small leap out of his comfort zone.

The young man running the ride packed us all in. We sat in the middle, facing a group of teenage girls who were whispering and giggling while pointing to the boys behind them. I remembered being that young. The last time I was on The Boat, I was the same age as those girls were now. It hit me how old I was. *Was it that long ago? I* was now the bouncing buoy in a sea of younger children.

As the ride began, I glanced at James. He seemed okay. The Boat ascended. The girls stopped giggling and started screaming. James held on tight to the bar in from of him and ducked, but I reassured him he was fine.

As the big swing up turned into the big swing down, I felt my stomach lurch. *Oh no.* The teens got louder. *Oh shit.* My guts were not having it and they were making it loud and clear. I started to burn up and a suffocating lump formed in my throat. All I could smell was teen body odour. I looked down at James and saw that he was beginning to laugh and throw his hands in the air. He was loving it. What the hell was *I* doing on this ride? The panic was multiplying fast. If I didn't get off soon, I wouldn't be able to breathe... or I'd throw up, at the very least. Those were my options. I stared in horror at the screaming girls in front of me. How could they be enjoying this ride so much? Up and down we went. The lights and blaring music of the amusement park began to blur as I scanned the room for the young man controlling the ride. There he was. I stared at him and began waving my arms in the air. He saw me and gave me a big smile. Then he nodded and gave me a thumbs up. *Fuck.* I tried again. I pointed to James again and motioned to stop the ride. His eyes widened and he understood this time as he laid on the control stick. The Boat began to slow and I could hear the riders' disappointment.

I heard grumbles around me. "Why are we stopping?" I averted eye contact with anyone and shrugged my shoulders. The ride finally came to a full stop and I walked off with James. I wasn't sure I could walk straight so I was glad he took my hand in his. He did not even notice that we had not been on long. As we walked away, I could hear someone say, "Oh, that little boy must have been sick. They had to get off." James didn't hear the comment and didn't notice me nodding in response to them. The ride started back up again as I scurried away as fast as I could.

Mark happened to be nearby. He saw me and his smiling face turned into concern. "Why are you all sweaty and red? Are you okay?"

"I'll tell you about it later." I could feel my face returning to its original colour.

"We went on the big boat!" James said.

Mark laughed a little. "Oh, you tried the Flying Galleon did you?"

I nodded, "Yes, yes we did. And it would have turned into the 'Flying Vomit' if I had not gotten off."

Mark and I went our separate ways once again. I was so relieved to be off the ride that I just followed James around, holding his hand like a docile zombie, letting him stand in line once again for the kiddie rides. I wasn't the one to teach James about being brave that day. I held his coat and waved at him as the mini-train made its way back to the station.

## SNAPSHOTS

Erin: "Maddie, I have a bully."

Me: "Oh yeah? What's his name?"

Erin: "Tommy."

Me: "Tommy sounds dumb. Tell him I said that."

Erin: "I can't say that."

Me: "Sure you can. Tell him your stepmom says he's a jerk."

Mark: "You really got this mothering thing nailed down, hey?"

# Chapter 12
# CHANGE YOUR PASSWORD

The September fall mornings required sweaters on the walk to school. The kids were settling into their new elementary classes and we were harvesting the last of our small garden.

Mark hired a lawyer and was fighting for sole custody. His ex-wife had been served. The affidavit our lawyer filed was thick and heavy, matching its emotional weight. The court date was just a few weeks away.

Erin was sitting on the porch playing with a friend when she saw a car pull up in front of our house. She ran inside, panicked. "Mom's here!"

I ran to the garage to get Mark. "She's fucking *here*!"

We both hurried into the house through the back door to see the kids standing at the open front door with his ex-wife leaning down to hug them. Mark stomped over and placed himself between her and the children. He pointed outside. "Beat it."

In all the years that I heard Mark converse with his ex on the phone regarding the children, he spoke calmly and did what he could to keep the peace. He didn't even challenge her when she swore in her emails that I would never spend any time with their kids. But in this moment, something was different, and it felt like time stopped.

We all stood there. Neither the children nor I were familiar with their inflamed dynamic.

His ex-wife cried out, "You're not even going to let me hug my kids?!"

He shook his head and said, "You cannot show up at my home unexpectedly. You can call me, and we can arrange a meeting."

We all continued to stand still looking at Mark for what would happen next.

She walked away, back to the car where her much younger boyfriend remained behind the wheel. Mark closed the door and turned to us, then looked down and crossed his arms. A few seconds later he took a breath, opened the door and said, "Go give your mom a hug."

They seemed confused but walked out the door. Mark and I watched them all hug her. We looked at each other and shook our heads in unison. What an emotional mess.

She opened the trunk of the car and gave the boys the toys that had been left behind when foster care had removed them from her. I stood at the open door watching them while Mark took a seat at the kitchen table. His eyes shifted while he clasped his hands together to steady himself.

As the children continued to run past me into the house to unload their stuff, they told me what they were carrying.

"This is my transformer!" James stopped to show me. "Do you want to hold it?"

"Sure," I said. The whole situation was surreal.

"Mom says the rest of my stuff is still in storage." He said.

She left with her boyfriend and told Curtis, Erin, and James that she'd be staying in the city and would be in touch.

She had found our home by tracking Erin's iPod.

Mark allowed her to see the kids a few times before the court date but set boundaries she could not cross. I sometimes wondered if she had forgotten that we were on opposing sides. During one phone call, she asked Mark if we would watch her cat for her.

"Mom says I'll get my stuff from storage soon." James told us after a visit.

For years when Mark visited the children on Vancouver Island, he asked where the gifts were, that he had bought them. "In storage." was always their reply. We never challenged this statement, but none of us ever saw the toys that were in storage again.

Mark pulled up a chair and sat down in front of James, taking his sons' hands.

"Buddy, there is no storage. Okay?"

James stared at his dad for a few seconds.

"Do you understand?"

"Okay." James said.

He never mentioned it again.

After two separate visits in front of the Court of Queen's Bench, a judgement was made in Marks' favour awarding him full custody. Mark let his ex-wife visit the kids one last time in the parking lot outside her motel room. She cried. The children did not. They said goodbye, and Mark gave her twenty bucks for smokes. She left town. After years of watching Marks' spirit broken and battered by a volatile system, he and the kids received justice.

# Chapter 13

# BACHELOR BRIAN

It was October and the days were getting shorter. Halloween was right around the corner waiting to rear its creepy head. Neighbours began decorating their homes with glowing skeletons and spooky orange and black lights. With so many kids on our block, you could feel the buzz in the air. They chatted about their Halloween costumes and organized groups for the big event. I watched the kids try on their outfits, giggling and talking about the fun they would have. Their eyes sparkled to match the high-end shiny costumes Mark bought them. I felt nothing. Why couldn't I get excited about it? That night, I thought back to the Halloweens of my childhood.

I had never embraced the spirit of the Halloween season. I did enjoy the anticipation of stuffing my face with chocolate and candy for a week since sweets were rarely kept in our house. But I never got to wear a cool Halloween outfit; it was a financial luxury my minimalist parents didn't buy into. My mom told us to use her make-up and hairspray and go as "Punk Rockers". We ended up looking more like toddlers who had been left alone with markers. This kept me on the sidelines of the school parties and set me up for never enjoying the holiday. However, I did have the thrill of dumping all the candy out of my pillowcase at the end of the night. The candy was the only reward though, because I also never liked anything scary.

Because we lived on the outskirts of a small town in a rather remote area, every year we had to drive in about a mile to do any real door-to-door trick or treating. Before heading home, we made one last stop at our neighbour's home, which held the most excitement for us.

Bachelor Brian was an older, thin, rugged looking man without a wife or children. He drove an old white pick-up truck and lived like a hermit in a dirty home where he invited us in for candy. Every few months, my sister Jennifer and I went sneaking around, tapping on his rickety screen door. While we waited, several cats hid around the dilapidated shed and the old rusted junk piles in his yard, peering out at us. He grinned as he opened the door. We made small talk and acted as though we simply came by to see how he was doing. Silly shy kids, asking him aimless questions. A minute or so went by and he said what we had been waiting to hear. "Would you like to come in? I think I have a little candy I could give you." We thought we were so clever, disguising our visits in hopes of getting a few goodies from him. We skipped back home a few driveways down. The packs of black jawbreakers bounced in our pockets while we threw chocolate-covered almonds in our mouths.

On Halloween, Bachelor Brian was the last stop of the night. My mom drove down his dark winding driveway. It was quiet and spooky with the lights off in his house: just the gleam of the moon shining down. We saw a long table with full bags of candy: a feast of mesmerizing treats. We could not wait to jump out of the car. We approached the table, our eyes glazed over in anticipation of all the colourful sugary treats. At that moment, Bachelor Brian came running out of the darkness with a crazy terrifying mask on, waving his hands in the air. We screamed, and laughed, and screamed again. As he got close, he took off his mask and gave a little chuckle. Then he told us that we could pick a bag of candy. A whole bag. I remember picking a bag that contained fifty suckers. They were all attached to one another in plastic covering and when I got home, I had to take the time to pull them all apart. Jennifer picked a bag of Molasses Kisses, each individually wrapped in orange paper with witches, pumpkins, and owls on them. I never understood how she liked them. They glued my mouth together and tasted horrible.

*****

Mark's sister had her annual Halloween party a couple of days after October 31st as it had fallen on a Thursday. It hadn't occurred to the kids until the day of the party to ask me where my costume was. I told them I didn't have one. They couldn't believe this. How could I not have a costume for the party? I felt tongue tied. I didn't want to tell them that I didn't give a shit about Halloween. My minimalist upbringing was holding strong and steady, telling me that it was ridiculous to buy a ninety-dollar costume that I'd just wear once. Mark said he would pay for it and I still refused. The kids seemed stunned. I stood staring at their flabbergasted little faces. I thought about Bachelor Brian and the spirit he had. I then thought about Mark telling me that since Halloween was over, the costumes would be half price. I got my party-pooper ass up and bought myself a costume. If Bachelor Brian—who didn't even have kids—could understand the importance of a fun Halloween and the happiness it brought to them, then there wasn't a good reason for me to opt out.

I picked out a Greek goddess costume, on sale for thirty dollars. I even put on make-up and made the effort to curl my hair, trying to match the theme of the flowy white and maroon outfit. Once I had it on, I discovered that I enjoyed pretending I was something that I wasn't for one night. We took fun pictures, and everyone indulged in large plastic bowls full of mini chocolate bars and small chip bags. The children danced to "The Monster Mash" in the living room while I joined Nicole and the Party Moms at the kitchen table. We drank wine and snacked while talking about husbands, boyfriends, and kids. We could hear the men cracking jokes in between conversations about football and tattoos. Once in a while, I saw Mark, in his Pirate costume, zoom through the kitchen chasing one of his nieces. A few times during the night, James or Erin came and sat on my knee.

Even though I had a fun night, I can't say it changed my views about Halloween. Curtis, Erin, and James seemed to appreciate my effort and I figured that was the most important part. In the following days, I could not help but think some more about Bachelor Brian. How did a bachelor know and care so much more about children's happiness than I did?

## SNAPSHOTS

"Okay, come down and kiss us goodnight. Me first. And don't forget to give me a good wet one!" -James

# Chapter 14
# EMERGENCY

The boys started to get into bathroom routines that were a little more normal. Mark and I constantly monitored them, and I insisted on seeing what ended up in the toilet bowl. As a nutritionist I spent a great deal of time counselling people about healthy bowel movements, so in this way, it didn't feel odd to want to see what was moving out of them. Were the laxatives and fiber drinks working? Hit and miss. Miss for a long time. Implementing a schedule that revolved around decent food, enough water, and scheduled bathroom trips seemed like a full-time job. If we didn't tell them to go and sit on the toilet after a meal, the boys might not think to go on their own, causing further constipation and avoidance. It was a continual burden. I could not wrap my head around the fact that they didn't appear to care one way or the other. After all else failed, prompting the boys with treats if they had a bowel movement in the toilet each day seemed to be the winner.

The amount of straining James did to produce a poop to get a treat was a little concerning. He deemed any little rabbit turd he pushed out a success and asked for a reward. I didn't argue. I wanted to keep him in the habit.

One Friday night, James called me into the bathroom as he often did when he was done, but this time his little face was frozen in terror. "What's wrong?" I asked, concerned.

"Something happened!" His voice high and trembling. He still had his little pants down and turned around to show me his backside.

I peered down and said, "Oh James, that's just poop that you need to wipe up."

"No! It's not, it's from inside of me!"

I took a step back to get a better view and my jaw fell. I had never seen such a thing. A university degree that had me studying so much anatomy, in addition to years in the wellness industry did not prepare me for this. I didn't even know this was possible. I realized that he had strained so hard that he had pushed part of his colon out and it was sitting there in a dark purple blob between his little bum cheeks.

I closed my mouth before he turned back to look at me. I mustered all the calm I could and kept my voice quiet. "Does that hurt?"

"No! It doesn't!" I saw he was shaking.

"All right, well that's good," I paused. "I think we will need to go to the hospital Emergency room tonight."

"I don't want to go to the hospital! Am I going to die?" Tears streamed down his face.

"No. You'll be okay."

I had no idea if he was going to be okay. I spoke in a soft tone, "How about I go get Dad, and we'll figure it out, okay?"

"No! Don't get Dad!"

I don't know why he didn't want Mark there. "I'll run you a warm bath and you sit in there and relax, okay?"

He agreed to this and as I ran the water, I convinced him that Dad should come and see so we could decide what to do. He got in the bath and I saw the fear in his face, but he didn't see mine. I backed myself out of the door with a close-lipped grin. "Don't you worry. I'll go get Dad. You relax."

I shut the bathroom door and shuffled over to Mark in the living room. He looked up at me from the couch. "What's going on in there?"

"Holy fuck!" I tried to whisper but failed. "James's colon came out of his bum!"

"What?" Mark sat up.

"Yeah! Part of his colon is out of his bum hole! It looks like a dark blob of poop, but it isn't poop!"

Mark's eyes narrowed.

"He said he didn't want you to see, but I convinced him to let you come in so that we could figure it out. Make sure you are super chill in there. He's already upset."

I followed Mark to the bathroom. We poked our heads in. James seemed more relaxed now but still worried.

"Hey buddy. What's going on?" Mark asked.

"There's something wrong with my bum," he said.

"It's okay James. Show Dad and we'll figure it out."

James stood up and showed Mark his backside. It took everything in me to appear calm. A mild look of concern covered Mark's face, "Hmmm… well, does it hurt?"

"No."

"Alright, Maddie and I will figure it out. You stay here and relax."

Mark seemed as cool as a cucumber. Maybe I was overreacting to this whole thing. Maybe Mark, being a parent for so many years before me, knew something I didn't. We shut the door. Then Mark looked at me with wide eyes and mouthed one word. "Fuck."

I realized that day what a great actor Mark was. We sat on the couch and stared at one another. "What do we do?" This conversation went on for a few minutes. We decided we had no choice but to bring him to Emergency. I told Curtis and Erin about the situation and explained what we were going to do. They didn't seem concerned.

James was still in the bathroom when I brought him his pajamas. I told him to go downstairs and sit on the couch with his siblings, relax, and watch a little TV.

A few minutes later as Mark and I got our jackets, James ran up the stairs yelling, "It went back up! It went back up!"

"What?" I said.

"I was sitting there and after a little bit, I felt it go back in!"

"That is awesome, James." I breathed a sigh of relief. "Okay, well… I guess you can go back downstairs and take it easy." I watched him run back down in his little Mario Brothers pajamas.

Mark and I collapsed onto the bed. After staring at the ceiling for a moment, I glanced over at him. "Parenting is not for the faint of heart." We laughed a nervous laugh.

## SNAPSHOTS

*Erin sits down beside me on the couch as I sip my coffee in silence*

"What are you doing?"

Me: "Nothing."

*Erin looks around for a minute and sighs*.

"It's quiet here. Why don't you go on the computer or something?"

Me: "Because I'm already doing something."

Erin: "What are you doing?"

Me: "I'm doing nothing."

# Chapter 15

# ANNOYING AIDEN

"What's up, Aiden?" I asked after opening the front door.

"Can James come out?"

"Not right now. He has some homework."

"Well, can I come in then?" He asked.

"Not right now, Aiden. How about I send him to your house when he's done?"

"When will he be done?" He appeared offended.

"I'm not sure. Maybe half an hour. I'll send him over when he's done."

Fifteen minutes later, Aiden knocked on the door and I had almost the same conversation with him again.

We lived across the cul-de-sac from Aiden. He had become good friends with James, so he often came by the house and knocked loudly— for far too long—while staring in the large window of our front door. I was often in the middle of cooking dinner so sometimes I hollered for James to answer the door. Sometimes James was in the middle of chores, so he told Aiden that he'd be a few minutes. Other children who came knocking seemed to understand this, but no matter what James or I told Aiden, he could not take no for an answer.

I asked Mark, "What's with this kid? Is he ever annoying. None of the other boys on the block act like him."

Every time James opened the door to his annoying face, I could hear Aiden rambling the same set of questions in a voice of pure disdain that only a nine-year-old can get away with. "What chores? Why do you have to do chores? Well, when are you going to be done? Why do your parents make you do chores? Why can't you come out right *now*?", and on and on until I called out, "James, tell him you have to go."

It was the kids' winter holidays and they were off school for two weeks. Annoying Aiden came to the door every day and my irritation grew every time. One day I noticed him walk up but instead of a flurry of knocks, he put his face up to our front door window and peered into our home like a peeping Tom. He didn't see me as I was the only one on the main floor and off to the side. He moved to a window beside the front door, put his mouth up to the glass, and dramatically began blowing on it and fogging it up. I could hear him making all kinds of disgusting noises. He sounded like a donkey in heat. That was it for me. I stomped to the door and sharply opened it, staring at him in disbelief.

He was a little startled by me. "Oh, hi James' mom. Can James come out?"

I thrust my jaw forward. "No, Aiden. James cannot come out right now. And I'll tell you something; you can't go around looking through people's windows into their homes. All right?!"

He looked stunned. "Oh. Okay."

"Fine!" I snapped. I shut the door and saw Erin behind me. She had seen the whole thing.

"Maddie, I know you don't care, but Aiden's walking away crying."

"What?" Fuck. Out the window I could see Annoying Aiden skulking back to his house with his head bowed. I turned back to Erin.

"Seriously? Was it like a little cry or a full out cry?"

"I think a full out cry."

Fuck.

I opened the door again, "Aiden!" I called out. He turned and glanced at me over his shoulder. The last thing I wanted to do was invite him in, but I felt like a monster for making him cry. I heard the words come out of my mouth. "Do you want to come over for milk and cookies later?" His face lit up. "Okay then, I'll send James over to get you in a bit."

I closed the door, took a deep breath, and walked to the kitchen to pull the flour out of the cupboard.

"Are you making cookies now?" Erin asked.

"Yep. Homemade gingerbread cookies," I said as I also reached for a wine glass and the bottle of cabernet I bought.

"The ones we love that take forever to make?" she asked.

*Frickin' Annoying Aiden.*

Erin reached for two aprons, "Can I help?"

## SNAPSHOTS

*Helping Curtis sign up for a card game site*

Me: "It needs a profile picture so I'll find one and add it for you."

Curtis: "Maddie, I think I should pick my profile picture. I know that you and Dad think you're cool and all, but, you know, you're kinda not."

# Chapter 16

# MERRY CHRISTMAS AND HAPPY NEW YEAR?

Mark plowed through the door a few weeks before Christmas with an enormous spruce tree and a giddy smile on his face. He was holding one end of the tree horizontally trying to manoeuvre it into the house while his buddy Derek held the other end. Mark had called in some extra manpower for this endeavour. Vibrant green needles flew everywhere as they squeezed the huge tree through the doorway.

We had not put up a tree since our first Christmas together five years ago. We didn't connect enough sentimental value to going through the effort of buying a tree every year and decorating it. But now we had the kids, and Mark was excited to make this an occasion they would remember.

I had rearranged the furniture in our small living room, but the tree was too big for the space. Mark and Derek stood in the living room holding the tree, grinning away.

"Where do you think we're going to put that Giant?" I asked.

"Over in the corner," Mark pointed to the small space I had cleared.

To humour Mark, I helped shuffle the tree to the corner. The Giant's head hit the ceiling and pieces of stucco and resinous needles rained down on us.

"Hmmm," Mark's smile turned to concern, "Let's get the saw!"

They spent the next twenty minutes bringing The Giant back outside and sawing down about a foot at the bottom. I swept up the needles.

Once The Giant was back in, he fit straight up in the corner. We cut the twine and he exhaled and stretched out his many green arms. He was secure. I poured myself a glass of wine and sat on the couch staring up at his twelve-foot height. He took up about twenty-five percent of our small living room. He had authority and seemed to declare: "I'm making up for all the years you didn't have a tree." I raised my glass, "Touché, Green Giant. Touché."

We turned on festive music. "I'm Dreaming of a White Christmas" by The Drifters played while we called Curtis, Erin, and James up. I watched their eyes widen as they looked up, way up. That night, the three of them took turns decorating The Giant with shiny new ornaments. They had mini meltdowns about whose turn was next, but they kept working together. An hour later the towering spruce had now softened; he was dressed up for the occasion. The kids insisted that I put the angel on top. I climbed onto our tallest chair barely managing to reach the tip of the tree. We plugged in the lights and thus began a new tradition.

Back in November we spent a lot of time shopping for presents. The minimalist in me cringed at the thought of spending so much and buying into the superficial marketing side of the holiday. I countered this with what I thought was the true meaning of the season: baking cookies and spending quality time with family.

Throughout many nights in December, we huddled together in the living room with the company of the fireplace and our friendly Giant. We watched Christmas movies and made loads of homemade popcorn. I bet the children they couldn't throw the popcorn up and catch it in their mouths. Popcorn flew all over the kitchen as we tossed piece after piece in the air and dove our mouths under. After Curtis won the race to three, we snuggled back in on the couch and watched a favourite classic, *A Christmas Story*.

New Year's Eve has always been one of my favourite holidays. I was excited to spend the evening with Mark and the kids. We bought them a new gaming console and the game, *Just Dance*. I figured if they were going to stare at a screen for hours, at least this would get them dancing their little butts off the couch. Plus, it would be perfect for our New Year's downstairs party!

The game came with a motion detector that monitored our movements. Whoever could imitate the dancers on the screen the best would win the round. Mark had a knack for winning most rounds! We spent all evening downstairs with them, watching each other try to dance and laughing together in good fun. We watched the countdown on TV and gave each other big hugs before going to sleep shortly afterwards.

It had been one full year since Erin had come to live with us, and what a year it had been. The depression that took hold of me during the summer lingered. But moments like this seemed to make the whole ordeal worth it.

\*\*\*\*\*

January arrived like a steamroller. The only time I felt the air in my lungs was when I meditated for twenty minutes a day or right before I fell asleep at night. Otherwise my breathing was shallow and quick, anxious. I could not shake the heaviness on my chest.

We were all in counselling now with our family psychologist, Dr. Mandel. Erin had lived with us for one year and the boys for over six months. They still needed to work through the present transitions and their past experiences. Mark and I needed help figuring out the best choices for them.

None of them were interested in talking with their mother on the phone when she called every few weeks. Curtis rolled his eyes and took the phone from Mark before proceeding through the obligatory short conversation.

Should we force them to talk with her? Mandel explained that it was not up to the kids to make adult decisions. Mark explained to his ex-wife that he was ending the phone calls while we were all getting therapy. There wasn't much resistance from her.

We had spent the fall and winter running around to Beavers, Girl Guides, and Scouts. These associations expected more than just dropping off and picking up a child once a week. Even though we paid for the three of them to attend, we were expected to volunteer. This included overnight winter camping trips. This required me to sleep on top of a cold bunk bed for a weekend, bundled up in my winter clothing with my sleeping bag zipped over my head.

We also helped fundraise. We had to sell a minimum amount hustling expensive popcorn; otherwise we would have to pay a fee. When we first participated in going door to door, collecting and sorting recyclable bottles and cans to earn money for the bottle drive, the boys weren't in uniform since they were still new. A man in an open garage stacked with pop and beer cans gave me a hard time asking to prove we were indeed from

Beavers. He offered us twelve cans in the end, with a comment: "Make sure you're in uniform next time." I didn't even want his stupid cans after the exchange, as though I had nothing better to do than spend a cold Saturday morning going door to door lying for a few aluminum cans.

We also sold cookies. I sent out an email to all of my colleagues letting them know I had chocolate mint cookies for sale. A co-worker of mine, a guy I liked who was young, had an abundance of energy, righteousness—and didn't have any children—replied to me with a long email. He explained that I was supporting a practice that went against my values. He pointed out at great length that the amount of refined genetically modified sugar and chemical mixture in these cookies was something I needed to think about and stop supporting. I was a nutritionist after all. He thought I'd see the light and urged me to revolt against the entire endeavour. As much as I understood his email, he didn't understand what I was going through. He wanted me to fight the system? Rage against the machine? I was more likely to punch him in the face. Maybe I would have had the strength and considered what he was saying a few years ago. Now I just wanted to make it through the day and bury my head in my pillow so the steamroller would stop, and I could feel myself breathe again.

## SNAPSHOTS

*Lunch at the table*

Curtis: "Did you know that herrings communicate through farting?"

If you had told me that my day-to-day would be spent having mass amounts of conversations about farting, I would not have believed you.

# Chapter 17

# HIDE AND SEEK

When you're searching for something that's gone missing and you have three children in the house it's hard to be sure if *you* lost it or if *they* took it. For one, they lie when you ask them. Or they honestly don't remember, so they say, "I dunno." The challenge becomes, do you believe *you* misplaced it and therefore search through kitchen drawers and under couches? Or do you suspect one of them took it and wait until it shows up in one of their drawers or underneath one of their beds?

I could not find the beautiful blue silk scarf that was a gift from my mom. I owned many scarves, so it was possible that I left it at work or simply misplaced it. I searched for days. It didn't make much sense for me to wear it since it was freezing outside and the material was delicate, but Mark and I were planning a date, so I wanted to wear my special scarf.

James came home from school that afternoon and started taking off his bulky winter coat as he chattered on about his day. Still rambling as he hung his coat on the hook behind him, he turned back towards me and I watched as his little hands shifted to his neck where he began unraveling his scarf. Or rather, *my* blue silk scarf. I watched as he grabbed at it and untwisted it from his neck. Once off, I noticed the two tight knots that he had added to the ends. He scrunched it into a ball and punched it into his coat arm and ran down the stairs.

It didn't seem to matter if I talked with them about it or not. Every day different things seemed to vanish. I began ignoring what I tried to think of as frivolous losses like different clothing accessories, my favourite suede boots, or my Crest white strips. Essentially, it was my mind I was looking for. I wondered if one of the kids had it hidden it their drawer or under their bed. Luckily, I did salvage my blue scarf.

I booked another appointment with Dr. Mandel.

## SNAPSHOTS

*Erin calling out from the basement*

"Maddie, I puked and it came out of my nose."

*Curtis walking in from school*

"My friend has a Megalodon shark tooth!"

Me: "Huh?"

"I'm serious. You should see it. It'll blow your nuts off!"

# Chapter 18

# MEXICO PART 2

It was February. Three years had passed since our first Mexico trip. To celebrate getting full custody of the kids, we booked another trip to Los Cabos. Just Mark, myself, and the children.

I liked flying about as much as I enjoyed driving through the mountains. Once on the plane, I placed a Lorazepam under my tongue and waited for the drink cart to come around. This still didn't prevent a small anxiety attack on our stopover. The kids had never seen me cry and I wasn't thrilled that they witnessed it. Head in my hands, sniffling, I saw them glance at Mark while staying quiet and shuffling their feet.

Once we were on our connecting flight and up in the air, a few members of the cabin crew began rushing up and down the aisles. A calm voice spoke over the intercom, "If there is a medical doctor on board, could you please raise your hand?"

I felt my heart beat hard and fast against my chest. I whipped my head over at Mark in the aisle across from me, widening my eyes and dropping my jaw so there was no doubt what I was feeling. He smiled and said, "It'll be okay. Don't worry about it."

Mark had a way of calming me down. I could not have been so brave in the last few years if it wasn't for him being so tough. His strength grounded me. He could pull me out from a downward spiral, look me in the eyes and say, "You're all right." And somehow, I believed him. I *was* always okay. Mind you, he also had moments where he drove me fucking crazy.

I sank down in my seat, dizzy in a prescription—and wine—induced haze. I turned my head and was now eye to eye with James. He grinned the way kids grin when they have no idea what is going on. He did that a lot. I knew he was just a little boy at eight years old, but he could not seem to read people much. Sometimes this gave me great frustration, but in times like these, it was pure gold.

He lifted up his favourite stuffed toy. "Do you want to hold my stuffy?"

"No, James. But thank you for asking," I said.

He held up his favourite book. "Can you read me *Skippyjon Jones*?" It was his favourite. Biker Nana had read it to him a hundred times. I didn't read it as well, he once told me, but he asked me to sit on the side of his bed and handed me the book every night anyway.

"Yes! Yes I can." I needed this distraction.

I'm not sure how well I read—or slurred—the book, but he didn't complain.

After settling into our resort, we reviewed the schedule for the week and saw that snorkeling was available as a tour. Mark and I chuckled, reminiscing about The Pirate Ship. Enough time had passed for us to find the whole excursion wildly funny. But as the tours filled up, snorkeling was one of the only choices left. Curtis and Erin seemed interested, even though we reminded them of the last time. We figured it couldn't hurt to ask the employees at the resort what to expect. To our surprise, they described a glamorous large yacht. There would be a nice lunch, drinks, an older crowd, and no pirates this time. We would start off with some whale watching, relax on the large deck, and then get in the water for some snorkeling. Although we were still reluctant, this did sound like a more sophisticated adventure compared to the rugged pirate fiasco. A little tamer and our speed; plus, we could enjoy the yacht and forego the snorkeling portion if we decided.

Similar to our first trip to Mexico, the tour bus dropped us off in Cabo San Lucas, located at the Southern tip of the Baja California Peninsula. Tourists walked the boardwalks of the marina in sunglasses and floppy hats while sea lions playfully swam around the boats. We snapped a few pictures. I felt optimistic.

We boarded the yacht and headed off into the clear blue ocean. An iconic landmark came into view, what the locals called, "El Arco" (the arch). This area is also known as "Land's End." There is a series of jagged rock formations, carved by nature, that marks this destination. This is where the Sea of Cortez, also known as the Gulf of Mexico, meets the Pacific Ocean.

Among the different rock shapes is a famous arch, and a formation that juts out at a sharp angle from the water, called Neptune's Finger. Pelicans fly above and rest on the rocks. There are also beaches in the area: the smaller sized Lover's Beach on the Sea of Cortez, where it's safe to swim in the calm waters; and the larger Divorce Beach that lines the Pacific Ocean where dangerous waves and strong rip currents are to be had.

Soon we saw some whales jumping in the distance. The crowd was impressed, and we all clapped. How wonderful and peaceful. I had a couple of glasses of wine and Mark, who didn't enjoy drinking alcohol and rarely had a sip, let loose and decided to have a couple of highballs.

We arrived at the location where the snorkeling took place and were feeling pretty good. Once again, my liquid courage set in and the kids began cheering on the snorkeling adventure. All of the guests who opted to go seemed excited. "What the hell!" I said. We suited up.

This time, instead of a plank, we were able to climb down a ladder into the water. I was off to a good start, but as soon as my toe touched the cold water a small flashback of the pirate ship gave me a jolt. Here I was, once again half drunk, beginning to wonder if I was making the same mistake.

Mark, Curtis, and Erin swam ahead of James and me. The swim was, once again, going to be a little long, but that was okay. Things seemed to be moving along all right until Erin yelled out, "I have something in my flipper. I'm taking it off."

"No. Don't take it off," Mark bellowed.

I could see Erin's hand surface out of the water holding her flipper.

"How big are the fish going to be?" Curtis asked.

"Curtis, I told you, they might be as big as last time." I could hear Mark getting frustrated.

I struggled with James to catch up to them, but they were quite far ahead.

"I don't know if I want to do this," Curtis shouted.

"What? We're already here. We're already doing it!" Mark was losing his cool. The wheels were coming off, yet again.

"I'm going to swim to the shore," Curtis yelled out.

Erin was struggling to swim and still had her flipper in hand.

Mark turned his head back and yelled out, "We're going to the shore."

"I'll meet you there." I gave him a wave.

Although James had developed a charming optimism in the last few months, with barely any swimming experience, he was not getting the hang of the flippers. I wasn't much better and was becoming exhausted trying to keep him going on this long swim. The lifejacket kept him afloat, but his skinny arms and legs were getting tired. I didn't even bother looking for fish at this point. We had branched away from the small group. "Let's swim to shore, James."

We arrived closer to the shore. Erin was sitting, crying and holding both flippers in her hands. Curtis and Mark were arguing about going back into the water. Curtis wanted a boat to come and pick us up. Mark was hollering as he waved his own flippers in the air. "Curtis! A boat will not come and pick us up. We have to swim all the way back to the yacht."

James and I tried to find our footing as we approached the beach, the ebb and flow of the ocean current was strong and difficult to navigate with our flippers on. We fell back and forth trying to haul our bodies onto shore. I took a flipper off to gain some foot control but realized there wasn't any soft sand beneath me. There didn't seem to be *any* sand. The whole floor before the beach area was covered in tiny sharp rocks. I told James to keep his flippers on, but we noticed the rocks working their way through them. We stumbled onto the shore in pain, collapsing, breathless.

A moment later, I assessed the situation. James started shaking the rocks from his flippers, Erin was whimpering, and Curtis was still trying to negotiate a boat ride back. Mark and I looked at one another in disbelief.

"Why did we do this again?" I asked.

"I don't know, because we're clearly stupid," Mark looked dumbfounded.

We both nodded, "Let's get back to the boat."

Twenty minutes later, after a lot more exhausted swimming, we arrived back onto the yacht. Feeling defeated, we cleaned up and tried to enjoy the rest of the ride back.

"Sorry we didn't see any fish, James," I said.

"We were supposed to see fish?"

"Yeah, what do you think we were doing out there?"

"I thought we were just swimming to the shore."

At least one kid wasn't disappointed.

James seemed like he was in deep thought. "Maddie, I've been thinking."

I leaned in for him to tell me.

"Who do you think would win a staring contest, a human or a stuffy?"

## SNAPSHOTS

Erin: "Why are you in bed this early?"

Me: "Because I feel horrible."

Erin: "Do you have a cold?"

Me: "Yes."

Erin: "Do you have a sore throat?"

Me: "Yes."

Erin: "What else?"

Me: "I think I have the flu. I need to rest in bed for now."

Erin: "I see. Yeah, I think you might have leukemia."

Me: "I don't think that I do."

Erin: "Well, do you have a headache?"

Me: "I think you might be giving me one right now."

Erin: "Okay, well, I'm gonna go play."

Me: "That sounds good."

Erin *walking away*: "I hope that you don't have leukemia!"

# Chapter 19

# THE CAN OF WORMS

The biggest coping strategy I had learned throughout my life was to laugh. This came in handy while trying to pull off being a decent mom. But my usual nature of finding the good humour to cope with a tough situation was manifesting into something else inside me. I was developing a Joker-like character beneath the surface. The maniacal arch enemy of Batman, The Joker, deranged and unpredictable was taking me over. Beneath my skin, just millimetres from every wrong move I made, was a green-haired lunatic. Poking at my skin, ready to laugh in a maniacal fit at the absurdity of what other parents might deem "normal". It was either that, or I broke down crying. Those seemed to be the only two faucets available these days. *Pick one.*

Reprieve came when the place where I work closed for renovations, which meant I was off work for three weeks. I had been managing staff four days a week while trying to keep up on tasks at home. Mark and I never seemed to catch up. The long list loomed and this was my chance to get a few things checked off.

It was time for the kids to go to the dentist. When I arrived, I told the receptionist that my kids were here for their check-ups. I preferred never to refer to them as my "stepkids". It sounded so formal and detached. I was caring for them full-time now; I didn't want the word 'step' to imply there was anything less.

After the receptionist called Curtis in, my phone rang. Erin and James played in a small toy room that the waiting area provided. I motioned to them that I was going to be outside for a minute. It was a co-worker on the other end. She asked if it was possible for me to come back to work earlier than originally planned. I immediately felt dizzy. I thought of all of the plans I had, *just* to catch up on everything that was falling behind: doctor's appointments, eye appointments, small home repairs that we couldn't keep up with; the list went on. This three weeks off was no holiday. It was a time when I had planned to catch up.

Not long ago, it was easy for me to take extra shifts. It was now hard for me to remember that there were times, before having the kids, that I didn't mind working six days a week, in addition to attending several training sessions a month to forever add to my knowledge of the natural health industry. I wore many hats at work and I could see why they were asking me to come back sooner.

My heart began to beat faster. "I can't. I just can't." I tried to talk calmly, but the panic must have seeped through the phone into her ear.

"It's okay," she said.

I was so thankful that the people I worked with were understanding and kind.

I walked back to the dental office feeling relieved, like I had narrowly escaped a sinkhole. I wondered, how did other parents do this? The expectations when working outside the home, parenting, paying bills, keeping your relationship with your partner healthy, and trying to keep yourself healthy: it seemed like an impossible endeavour. Is this why so many people I knew took prescription medicine, as well as other forms of mood altering drugs?

When all three kids were done, the dentist came out. She sat next to me, leaning in, and very gently said, "We had to go overtime on cleaning James' teeth. He had a lot of build-up in the front." She hesitated. "I'm wondering, does he brush his teeth, at all?"

I was so embarrassed. Did he brush his teeth? He still hadn't mastered bowel movements in the toilet. We had him in the largest size of Pull-Ups since the prolapsed bowel incident. The doctor said he wasn't allowed to 'push' for a few months. Never mind the basic additional skills like tying up shoelaces and doing up a zipper and button on a pair of jeans. Curtis and James fought to continue wearing Velcro shoes and sweatpants. It was a constant battle getting them to evolve from their established habits.

I almost teared up. The Joker got a real kick out of this. He laughed and laughed inside of me and said, "Can I please open the can of worms?" Part of me wanted him to grab the can, snap the clip back, and begin peeling it open. Pink worms with tiny mouths would fly all over the room; screaming out random comments: "She can't keep up! She's confused all the time! She's going fucking crazy!" They would bounce off the dentist's lovely glasses and land all over the carpet in her formal and proper office space. My mouth would deform into a painted red smile. I'd laugh in hysterics as I leaned back to begin doing the backstroke in the pool of worms.

Instead of taking the plunge, I pushed the Joker back down below the surface. I clenched my hands to hold both faucets shut.

I looked at the dentist, defeated. "I don't know how much he brushes." As much as I hated saying I was their "stepmom", here it was: the only card

I had left to play so I wouldn't feel like such a failure. "I'm their stepmom," I said. "I'm trying, but it's taking time."

An understanding came across her face. "Oh, yes. I get it. It's hard. You can't micromanage them all the time. You can only do your best." She was kind. Maybe she saw a glimpse of the Joker in my eye.

"Thank you for saying that. It *is* hard. I can't police everything they do. It would be a full-time job."

Her sympathy made me feel a little better. Sometimes moms need someone to give them a break from beating themselves up.

## SNAPSHOTS

*Lying with Erin on the couch*

Erin: "I'm going to find a bottle, and I'm going to fart in it, and then I'm going to cork it and throw it into the ocean, and then someone will find it, open it and say, "Oh my God! It's a fart."

Me: "You're gross."

Erin: "And I'm going to send a note in it that says, "From Maddie Laberge."

# Chapter 20
# DINKS

I needed to get away for a day. I texted my friend Sophie.

Sophie and I had worked together for a few years and even though she is seven years younger than me, we had a lot in common and connected when we met. We spent quite a bit of time together before I became a stepmom. Whether it was having a glass of wine at a local bar, sitting on a patio getting some lunch, or making good on an invitation to her parent's cabin, Sophie and I always had fun and loved getting together. It had been a few months since we'd last seen one another. She was now living with her boyfriend Liam, and I was immersed in the responsibilities of my family life.

Before contacting and suggesting an outing with Sophie, Mark and I planned for it for an entire week; I'd make plans for a Saturday between 11:00 a.m. and 4:00 p.m. This would give me plenty of time to socialize with Sophie while Mark stayed with the kids. Sure, I wouldn't be home for regular Saturday chores, but I rarely made plans to see friends. After some careful rearranging we would make this work for me.

All week I anticipated getting out of the house and having some fun. I could not wait to catch up. We weren't even sure what we were going to do. We never made plans about where to go beforehand. We waited to be in the moment. When Saturday came, I hopped out of bed like it was Christmas morning. I counted down the minutes, waiting until 10:00 a.m. to text her.

"What do you feel like doing?" I wrote.

I waited a few minutes for a reply. It was unlike her not to respond right away.

"Hey, do you think we could make it for another day? Liam and I are so hungover."

My heart sunk. I couldn't believe it. I stared at the message, re-reading it. I slumped into my chair, frustrated. She had no idea what I went through to make this work. I didn't blame her. She and Liam didn't have children. They led a different life. Mine had become one of strategic planning to acquire a few hours of my own to go out and play.

I took a deep breath. I needed to let Sophie know. I realized this was a pivotal moment in our friendship. Our relationship had changed and maybe now, the friendship would not carry on. It wasn't only *my* life and *my* time any longer. I was responsible for so much more. The person I was when I had first met Sophie, was gone. I thought for a minute about it, then I texted back.

"That's fine, Sophie. But I want you to know, it took a lot of planning for me to get out of the house and have a visit. So next time we make plans, they have to go through."

Another few minutes went by. I wasn't sure how she would respond.

The text came through. "How about if we meet at my parents' and sit in their hot tub?"

"YES!" I rummaged through my drawer to find my bikini, got ready, and kissed Mark as I ran out the door.

I arrived and we gave each other a hug. She told me how bad she felt for trying to cancel. She didn't realize the planning it took on my part. I was so relieved she understood. I told her that it was okay. I was just happy to be out.

It was March and the weather was still cold and cloudy. I could see she had poured me a glass of red wine. We stripped down to our bathing suits, and in true Canadian fashion, threw a toque on our heads and lowered our bodies into the hot water. The heat felt so comforting. We sipped our drinks and it felt like old times. There was a peace and serenity in the air.

Maybe the person Sophie knew before I had the kids wasn't gone. A few tiny snowflakes floated in the quiet light breeze in front of my face and I closed my eyes. And for a couple of hours, all my responsibilities faded, and I felt like my old self again.

# Chapter 21

# DAD

I watched Mark snatch Erin up and throw her on the couch. He tickled her and she shrieked; half laughing, half trying to catch her breath. She wiggled her way out of his grasp and tried to run past him, but she'd let him catch her and throw her again and again.

This was a typical weekend morning. The kids never knew when Mark would grab and toss them on the couch or over his shoulders. He often wrestled with them downstairs. I heard the hollering through the floor, unsure at first if there was an argument happening, or if they were messing around and body slamming each other. I opened the basement door to see Mark on all fours, with the kids attacking him one at a time. Periodically he raised his head and interrupted the game saying, "You okay?" They always were. I don't remember my dad ever asking me if I was okay.

The earliest memory I recall of my father is a good one. I must've been quite small, maybe two years old. He lifted me up, twirled me upside down and held me up just close enough for my feet to touch our low ceiling. He walked me along as I made the motion of tiptoeing on the ceiling of our small house.

In the first few years of my life I remember my dad as a gentle, yet strong, six-foot, two-inch man with receding dark hair. Because he was a mechanic, he often smelled of motor oil. When he wasn't dressed up to attend the church in our town, he wore a faded blue work shirt. The front pocket housed his square, dark-rimmed glasses along with a pen and a container of snuff.

I have many memories of my dad from when I was very young. Our family often went for long drives a few hours from our acreage, to the southern parts of Manitoba. We ended up driving down someone's long gravel driveway lined with tall trees. At the end was an open area that revealed a friend or relative's modest country home. Inside, there was sure to be a homemade cake or pastries with a glass of milk for the kids and coffee for the adults.

One summer, in the middle of a typical Manitoba heat wave where the temperature produced beads of sweat on our faces that were only relieved by the gusts of wind through the open car door windows, I sat nestled between my siblings in the backseat as my dad drove. There weren't any seat belts back there so the four of us crammed ourselves in.

My mom sat in the front as my dad drove down a dirt road that seemed like it was in the middle of a field. The grass was tall, dry, and blond in colour. It surrounded the road making the tracks barely visible. A loud buzzing noise came up around us and my mom was startled as a grasshopper flew into her open window. I was just tall enough to peer over the front seat to see through the windshield at what seemed like dozens of grasshoppers jumping from left to right, dancing in front of our slow-moving car. Their chirping song rang out in the quiet country air. Many landed inside the car. My parents and the rest of us all tried to shoo them back out the windows as we laughed.

At the end of this road was one of their friends' homes. As usual, after we kids indulged in the table of homemade goodies, we were the ones shooed outside to play with the children who lived there.

The best gift my dad gave me was the ability to find beauty in what he said God created. From admiring those grasshoppers in the bright sunlight to watching the brilliant orange flames roar in our fireplace during the wintertime, he believed there was magic to be found in our unembellished life.

He was a creative man and loved woodworking, making everything from our swing set to our couch and beds frames. He constructed a hen house for the chickens, geese, and ducks we kept and built a small two-storey barn which became my brother John's little abode. A tree house he constructed was about fifteen feet high in a huge old elm tree near our front yard.

My dad always wanted to build and invent things. But instead of listening to my mom's suggestions to add a much-needed addition to our small home, he built another, bigger barn, near the back of our property.

He liked to spend time in the yard, showing us how things worked. He taught me how to use his BB gun. I spent hours shooting at milk cartons that were weighed down with rocks. I remember how patient he was. One year he constructed a zip line for us kids that ran from the big barn to the house. None of us were ever injured on it, but my friends had to get their parent's permission before leaping from the second story barn door and experiencing the unpredictable ride.

Unfortunately, our simple life became *too simple*. Among many things my dad deemed unnecessary was a proper bathroom. We had a small bathtub, but we never had a flush toilet. We had a portable square camping toilet, made of hard plastic that my dad carried and emptied in the outhouse. With a family of four children, I'm sure this was a time consuming and unpleasant process. Sometimes it wasn't emptied and we had no choice but to run back and use the outhouse. In the summer I feared spiders crawling onto my privates, and in the winter it was cold and uncomfortable. An inconvenience for sure, but as a child, I don't remember complaining about these things. We grew up with what is normal to us, and that was normal. I now wonder what the hell he was thinking.

My mom *was* able to convince him to get a functioning washing machine after I was born, her fourth child. There was also the success of convincing him to buy a small black-and-white television a few years later.

When I was eight or so, I sometimes noticed my mom crying with my oldest sister consoling her. It was years later that these puzzle pieces of my young life formed a more complete picture for me: the depressing brown paneling on the walls in a home that was too small, in addition to the embarrassment of our toilet when company visited was something I believe my mom *wanted* to try and overlook long term. And she did, for years. She loved my father for most of their marriage. But the strict practices of the Catholic Church and the constant contributions my father made on Sunday, topped with his unreliable work ethic, left her insecure. He wouldn't let her get a job or a driver's license. Years passed and she was fed up with hiding the birth control pills that kept her from getting pregnant, but made her ill. There were only so many times she could ignore the whistles he directed at other women in her presence.

I imagine my dad was dissatisfied or had unresolved issues as I saw his anger and resentment develop and direct towards my mom. My mother—who was soft, kind, and gentle—began to harden. Quietly, she became our pillar of strength, protecting us from understanding the verbal venom my dad threw at her and hushing him or taking us away to relatives in the middle of the night. Eventually he chipped away at her so often that cracks began to form.

Nearing the end of their marriage, my dad—now diagnosed with schizophrenia—was someone I didn't know. A strange outrage flooded the house on Saturday mornings. This seemed to be the day we awoke to the most swearing and hatred. I realized I couldn't invite my best friend to sleep over anymore; the embarrassment and fear of the fights were too common now. My dad always stormed out afterwards, slamming the door.

A memory still runs through me sometimes: nine years old, waking up to shouts and then the sound of something breaking. I waited for my dad to finish screaming and leave before I walked out of my bedroom, to find my mom crying on her knees, cleaning up a shattered glass thermos that was filled with the hot coffee she had made for him.

There were many years that my dad warmed our home with a blazing fireplace. Then, there were mornings that he walked away from all of us, before stoking the fire, leaving only embers. It should have come as no surprise to him when the house he left cold, finally snuffed out the last small flame in my mom's heart. They separated when I was ten.

My dad wasn't present in my life much after my mom left him. It took me years to think of—and accept—the right word to describe our relationship and infrequent visits. *Incomplete* describes them both well. I'm not sure how much of it was the schizophrenia or how much of it was his lack of awareness as to what a father was supposed to be like with his children, but the end result always left me with a feeling of insecurity. I stopped trusting that my dad knew what to *do* and the resulting weight of responsibility falling on my own, unprepared shoulders was a lot to bear.

I remember an outing with him a year or so after my parent's separation. Because he was a car mechanic by trade, my father often frequented machine shops and car junkyards. I was eleven years old one time I went with him. It was just the two of us and he let me run off on my own. In and around cars, I played and hid. I came across a windshield that had large holes in it. Although the windshield had shattered areas, the remaining glass lay mostly intact, the cracks taking the shape of large cobwebs. I reached out and broke off a chunk. I held it in my hands and snapped apart the webbed glass. I played with it while I walked around until the glass suddenly punctured my finger. The sting frightened me. Drops of bright red blood appeared and tears filled my eyes. I looked up to see where my dad was. He wasn't in my sight. I was embarrassed that I had done this and I wanted to hide it from him. I felt silly. I didn't know what to do. The blood kept running down my finger and was now streaking the palm of my hand. I couldn't hide it. I wiped the tears away and went to find him. When I came across him talking with the owner, I bowed my head and told him I cut myself a little. Calmly, he walked me over to the owner's trailer that had an office and a bathroom. He told me to go inside and run it under water. I shut the door just in time for the tears to escape my eyes. I felt unsure of how to take care of this on my own. I wanted him to be there for me. I wished he knew what to *do*.

The bathroom was small and dirty and smelled like gasoline. I leaned over the tiny sink, running my finger under the cold water. The water diluted the blood as it ran into the filthy stained sink. A light auburn tinge began to appear over the gray residue. I felt nauseous and light headed. The smell of rusted metal and oil was overwhelming. I thought I was going to pass out so, I wrapped my finger in toilet paper and held it tight. I sat on the unwashed floor, with my back against the wall. I stayed for a few minutes until I could compose myself. Eventually I opened the door. I walked up to my dad once again and the owner handed me a couple of Band-Aids. We got in the car and he drove me home to my mom.

The visits were few and far between in the years that followed. He didn't offer much of anything to me. But due to my mom's insistence that I phone him and invite him out, we met up every so often for a McDonald's ice cream cone. I never knew what to talk about and the awkward silence always made the ice cream treat taste not quite as good as it should. He sometimes invited me to go to a church where they held prayer meetings. I agreed only because he sat in a group talking about the bible and drinking coffee while I was able to sit off to the side and eat cookies.

I tried to give him a school picture when I was in the seventh grade, but he handed it back to me, saying he didn't need it. Many years later I called him when I received my acceptance letter to university. He said it sounded complicated and that I shouldn't bother. Even though on some level I began to expect these types of comments, they never became easier to hear.

While I was still a teenager, a plug-in portable heater started a fire that tore through our family home that my dad still resided in after we had all left him. I still remember walking back into the house and smelling the odour of the burnt wooden beds he built all those years ago. A painting of a saint my uncle had made for us still hung on the wall, blackened and almost unrecognizable. Never having insurance on the house and being on disability due to his mental illness, my dad was forced to move to the city.

I still love my dad. I've long let go of any expectations. I visit him every so often in his bachelor suite in Winnipeg. He keeps his windows closed year round and his walls have yellowed from the trapped cigarette smoke. One wall displays years' worth of Christmas cards hung together with scotch tape. A large crucifix hangs above his small kitchen table, another hangs around his neck.

I watch as he sits, content and numb. He sips his whisky. He tells me that the bed bugs are gone now, but you never know, they could always come back. I look around his 'home'. His twin bed is covered with an old torn quilt, right next to a dusty desk with an old lamp. I ask him if he needs anything and if he's okay. He always says that he has all that he needs. He holds his drink and stares off and I look at his left hand. The same familiar hand I've seen for years. Half of his middle finger is missing from a work accident over thirty years ago, when we still all lived in the country house.

Now an old man, his softened brown eyes glance at me. He'll read the bible tonight, like every night, before turning off the lamp. I can hear the familiar certainty in his voice when he talks to me about religion. God's been good to him, he says. He hopes he doesn't live too long though. And in an awkward way, he gives me a shy laugh.

# SNAPSHOTS

*Rushing to an appointment while talking to the kids sitting in the backseat of the car*

Them: "What are we doing for Easter!?"

Me: "I don't know. I used to go to church and celebrate the resurrection of Jesus Christ."

Them: *Silence*

Me: "Why? What do you guys want to do?"

Them: "Can we have an Easter egg hunt?"

Me: "I guess. Is that what you usually do?"

Them: "And we paint eggs!"

Me: "Are you serious? That sounds like a lot of work."

Them: *Silence*

# Chapter 22

# BLAST OFF

It was June and a warm summer's evening had the sun still shining bright at 7:00 p.m. With a glass of wine in hand, I watched through the front door window as the neighbourhood boys and girls played outside. Chasing each other around in the cul-de-sac, they laughed and screamed. Sometimes they fought. It was like watching a wildlife show. I was starting to predict some of their interactions. I hated the noise that penetrated the house from their high-pitched howls, but there was something I enjoyed about watching them, too.

I was fascinated by the range of their emotions. The imbalance. As though they all had a mental disorder called Childhood. They were manic one moment, jumping high into the air with arms outstretched, like a rocket launching out of this world with pure euphoria. Blast off! Then as quickly, they could descend into despair, tumbling down in tears.

I strived for simplicity in my life and in my psyche. I could not imagine dealing with these kinds of erratic highs and lows that I witnessed outside my window.

James and Annoying Aiden aimed plastic guns at one another and every so often they clumsily fell down and wrestled on Aiden's front lawn.

Their energy seemed to know no bounds.

I wondered, as I took another sip of my wine, when did I stop chasing moments of 'Blast Off' happiness? Would I even recognize a 'Blast Off' moment these days? It seemed like life was just about finding my footing. If I stayed grounded, keeping my emotions as linear as possible, maybe I could make it through the day all right.

The alcohol helped by dulling my mind chatter. I knew logically that alcohol was a depressant but following a stream of logical thinking wasn't helping in my situation. Many things that should have been logical were not. And by that logic, I continued buying bottles of wine. I was much nicer to everyone after a glass or two. Our family psychologist didn't agree that this was the best method to use. I was also concerned because I knew he was right. I didn't know how else to cope.

James ran up the steps and I moved back before he flung open the front door. With grass stains on his knees, dirty hands, and messy blond hair, he gasped, "Can Aiden sleep over tonight?"

James had never asked this before, so it caught me a little off guard, "I don't know. I'll talk to Dad, I guess."

"Okay," James nodded, staring at me for a moment before running back outside. "My stepmom's gonna ask my dad!"

I was getting used to Annoying Aiden over the last few months. At times we had him over for lunch or a short visit so he could play video games with James. I guess The Joker in me had moments where he softened.

I went to the garage where Mark was cleaning up. "James wants to know if Aiden can sleep over."

Mark shrugged, "I guess."

With zero feeling on this one way or another, I walked back to the front door and called for James who was across the street in Aiden's yard. He came running as soon as he heard my voice.

I took another sip of wine. "Okay, Aiden can stay over tonight."

James' eyes widened, as though I told him he won the jackpot. He turned towards Aiden who was watching from his yard and yelled, "You can sleep over!"

Aiden began shaking and jumped into the air while yelling back, "Okay, wait there, I'll ask my dad!"

*Holy shit. Blast Off!* Their exchange was supercharged. I thought they might pee their pants. *They're that excited?*

Like a semi-obedient dog waiting for a treat, I watched James shuffle his feet back and forth while he waited beside me for Aiden to reappear. Thirty seconds later, Aiden came racing out of his front door. As he bolted across the street to meet James, he was so electrified that one of his shoes went flying off and soared about six feet into the air above his head. He didn't even notice.

"My dad said yes!"

He reached James and both boys began talking at the same time. They walked back to Aiden's yard as they discussed their plans for the night ahead. I heard the word "LEGO" a lot.

Aiden still hadn't noticed that he had just one shoe on and walked right past the other on the street.

I just witnessed an eight-year-old boys' version of Blast Off happiness.

That night, we made popcorn, and all watched the movie *Stand by Me*. James threw a blanket on the floor in front of the couch where Mark and I sat. He and Aiden sat shoulder to shoulder while questioning how a young River Phoenix could be smoking cigarettes. Mark and I gave each other a knowing look. Both of us had smoked cigarettes at fourteen, but we weren't about to tell them that.

Both boys glanced over at us whenever the young actors swore, which was often. It was as though they knew this movie was a little over-the-top for their age. They giggled at the taboo.

When the movie was done, we told the boys to get ready for bed. As they ran down the stairs, Aiden threw his arms up and yelled out, "This is the best night of my life!"

James shouted out his favourite part from the movie: "Chopper! Sic Balls!"

## SNAPSHOTS

*Sitting on the porch drinking wine. Curtis walks
out and sits on the step next to me*

Curtis: "I'm bored."

Me: "I'm never bored. In fact, I would love to be bored. A lot of
adults are never bored because when they're sitting in the quiet,
they still have their "to do" list going on in their heads."

Curtis: "Well, I can help you with that! All you have
to do is think about what *you* want to think about, not
what other people want you to think about."

# Chapter 23

# FIVE-DAY FAMILY VACATION

A couple of weeks into July, Mark and I figured we should plan a family holiday, but we didn't know where. The kids were already getting into a groove of sleeping in and sitting around in the basement. We wanted to go somewhere easy, familiar, and relaxing. Cheryl invited us to her home on Vancouver Island. She also offered to keep the children for the summer. All I could say was, 'Hell, yes. When do we leave'?

Although I was excited to go, I told Mark there was no way I was mentally able to be a passenger for two days through the mountains with him and the kids. To avoid being riddled with travelling anxiety, we arranged it so that I'd fly to the Island with his sister, Nicole. She was lucky enough to be granted a vacation away from her husband and children this time. Nicole and I could spend some time with Mark's mom beforehand, doing things that Mark had no interest in doing. Then he and the kids would arrive a couple days later. We had been together long enough for both of us to know this would be a better start to our vacation. I agreed that after our week was over, I'd travel back home in the car with him.

We packed our bags.

## DAY ONE:

Cheryl and her new younger boyfriend were waiting to pick Nicole and me up at the airport when we landed. The air was fresh, and we were thrilled to be there. We stopped to have lunch. As we filled our forks with the first bites of our salmon salad, Cheryl told us that a man was renting her camper so we would not be able to sleep in there. Mark and I usually stayed in there when we came with the kids since her loft was quite small. Instead, she said she had a surprise waiting for us. I never liked surprises, so when we stopped at the liquor store, I made sure to buy an extra bottle of "Surprise wine" in case I needed it.

The sun was still high in the sky once we arrived at Cheryl's place. Nicole and I grabbed our luggage, but instead of bringing our bags upstairs to the loft, Cheryl guided us under the stairs and around the corner of her home.

"Since I don't have the dogs anymore, I made this whole outdoor area into a new livable space. See? This is where you'll be staying," she gestured like a game show hostess, showcasing a prize.

Nicole and I walked into the space. It had once housed a long row of kennels for her dog breeding business. Now the dogs and kennels were gone, and the concrete had been cleaned and painted. A long kitchen table with chairs and outdoor loungers were placed at one end and a TV at the other. A hard, plastic roof covered the area, but no walls had been erected. She had set it up beautifully.

"Wow, this is really something, Cheryl," I checked out all the hard work she had put in.

She walked us over towards the TV that had a curtain hanging behind it. She drew the curtain to the side. This revealed a double bed that was surrounded by curtain panels on all sides. "See how cozy it is? You guys are going to sleep great out here."

I pointed to the bed, "We're sleeping outside?"

"Surprise!" She clasped her hands in front of her chest.

At that moment we heard some loud squawking sounds.

"Oh, that's nothing. It's only the chickens on the other side," she tossed the second panel aside and revealed her chicken coop approximately two metres from the bed, filled with over thirty-five birds.

Cheryl kept laying hens and one rooster. A handwritten sign and a small drop box sat at the end of her driveway. For those who wanted to purchase the full cartons she left out, the honour system was in place. After she discovered the box of cash had been stolen a few times, she gave up on the wholesome endeavor and just shared the eggs with family and friends.

"They get a little noisy in the morning. You have to let them out of their cage. No big deal. Let's go upstairs and get a drink!" She walked away.

Nicole and I stood there holding our luggage looking at each other until we began mirroring a small grin. I gave a little laugh, shrugged my shoulders and said, "We're sleeping beside the chickens."

"Yeah," Nicole said, "Let's get a glass of wine."

I don't remember much about that first night because I drank a lot of my "Surprise Wine." I remember falling asleep with my head under the blankets. I found out that Nicole opened the coop for the chickens in the morning to let them out so they could wander around the yard. I didn't hear them.

## DAY 2:

That evening Mark was set to arrive with the children. From the deck outside of the loft doors where we were all indulging in snacks and drinks,

I saw him pull up past the gate. He got out and appeared tired and angry. This was not a good start to our holiday. I walked down the stairs to greet them. After giving Curtis, Erin, and James a quick hug, they ran up to greet Nana and Auntie Nicole.

I approached Mark. He was leaning against the car with his arms folded, looking down to the ground. "What's up?" I asked.

"That was exhausting." He went on to tell me about the long road trip and several stops. They were one of the last cars to board the ferry from Vancouver to Nanaimo. Doing the two-day trip was a lot to handle and had cost a lot of money.

I felt bad. This didn't seem like the best time to tell him that we were sleeping outside. I encouraged him to leave everything in the car and come upstairs to relax for a bit.

A few minutes later, as I was busy getting the kids a snack in the kitchen, I noticed Mark had disappeared. I walked out to the deck and saw him standing in front of the camper door with his luggage.

The camper door flung open and a thin grey-haired man appeared. He sipped a beer.

"Hello," the man said as he leaned in the doorway.

"Hi. Who are you?" Mark asked without smiling.

"I'm Henry. Who are you?"

"I'm Mark, Cheryl's son. We usually stay in this camper."

"Oh. Well, I've been renting it for a few months. She didn't tell you?" He wrinkled his forehead and pushed his glasses up.

"Nope. She sure didn't," Mark turned his head as he noticed me walking towards him.

I pulled one of his suitcases. "I'll show you where we're sleeping," I said.

Cheryl overheard me and came down to show Mark the new area.

"Oh, you'll love it." She held onto her beer as she showed him around.

He didn't look thrilled but nodded in appreciation anyway.

Mark was never exactly excited or open to new experiences when we traveled. He liked his home, his bed, and his midnight peanut butter sandwiches and granola bars. He especially liked his sound machine that played the soothing drum of rain when he slept. Any holiday we took was a gamble. He felt an obligation to his family, though, and he mostly vacationed for the kids.

Judging from past travels, I wasn't much better, but I was trying to be more flexible and make the best of surprise situations.

Mark was checking out the bed. "We're sleeping outside?"

"Nicole and I slept out here last night. It was nice."

Cheryl guzzled her beer. "Make yourself at home, Markie!" Then she disappeared around the corner.

I cringed as I pulled back the other curtain to reveal the chickens.

Mark sighed. "I don't think they're going to sound as soothing as my rain machine."

"Why don't we ever remember to bring that thing with us?" I said.

Dusk descended and we decided to get settled in early. All of the sleeping arrangements were figured out. Even though it was cramped, I envied the kids and Nicole who were preparing to snuggle into the large pull-out couch up in the loft. The sun faded behind the tall trees and I noticed that familiar cold chill I usually developed in the mountains. I also noticed something else. A mosquito.

"Since when are there mosquitos here?" I asked Mark.

"There aren't, usually." We crawled under the covers and an annoying buzz rang in my ear. I swatted at my head. Then again.

"There are fucking mosquitoes out here," I whispered. "I didn't notice any last night."

"This sucks." Mark was as frustrated. I knew neither one of us could do anything about the bugs.

I sat up and reached for my suitcase. I pulled out my sweater and put it on with the hood up, drawing the strings together. Only enough space for my mouth and nose remained open. Luckily, sleep came fast.

## DAY 3:

Without opening my eyes, I could tell that the sun was rising. The chickens began squawking quietly at first and then, progressively louder. I heard Mark open their cage door. It helped bring their noise level down and once again we were able to doze off. Hours had passed and again I awoke to unfamiliar sounds. This time it was men's voices. I didn't recognize the voices, but this wasn't unusual. Cheryl was a social butterfly and she enjoyed having company at all hours. It was common for her friends to just drop in.

Mark was already out of bed, so I laid there for a moment wondering what time it was. Early, I sensed. As someone who has never been an early riser, I could usually sense it was still early without looking at a clock.

I hoped the washroom in the loft was empty so I could freshen up. I tossed the curtains back from the bed and saw Henry from the camper sitting at the long table having a beer. A younger man sat with him.

I shuffled out of bed. Walking by I muttered, "Good morning, Henry." Not feeling as well rested as I had hoped, I greeted the other guy.

He gave me a little wave, "Hey. I'm Michael."

I stopped for a few seconds and wiped the sleep from my eyes.

"And this is Annabelle."

He pointed to the medium-sized dog sitting beside him. Her big blue eyes watched me as she tilted her head to the side. She had the demure demeanour of a reincarnated Southern Belle. I nodded and made my way upstairs.

Erin and the boys ran around while Cheryl and her boyfriend whipped up breakfast.

"Good morning, Maddie. How did you sleep? Mark took the car to the store to get a coffee, you know how he likes to do that when he's here. I don't know why because we have coffee here, but he goes anyway."

Mark did this because he said his mom's coffee tasted like water. He liked his coffee as strong as rocket fuel and as thick as mud. Another thing he always missed about home: reliable robust coffee that jump-started his adrenal glands first thing in the morning.

I gave each of the kids a hug and walked past the fold-out couch to the washroom. I realized I left my bag with all my toiletries downstairs. I rinsed my face anyway and glanced in the mirror. I looked horrible and could not wait to take a quick bath and get ready for the day. I needed my bag, though.

Halfway down the stairs, I stopped when I heard someone yelling at Annabelle. The sweet little Belle came running around the corner with something in her mouth. I rubbed my eyes to be sure. Yes, it was a chicken.

Michael came around the corner. "Annabelle! You drop that chicken!"

Everyone else rushed out of the loft to see Michael chasing his dog in circles with the bloodied bird flopping in her jaws. Finally, she stopped.

"Drop it," he ordered. Annabelle reluctantly obliged.

"Oh no," Cheryl gasped and covered her mouth as she watched her bird lay lifeless.

The kids shrieked. "Go back inside, you guys. It's okay." I said, pointing to the door. As Cheryl ushered them in, she raised her eyebrows and shrugged. She had a knack for getting over disappointments right away.

I continued down the stairs and tried to ignore the situation. I found what I needed and headed back while Michael passed me holding the dead carcass. Annabelle was now on a leash and licking her chops.

Cheryl didn't have a shower installed but did have a big soaker tub. Some clean water and shampoo and I would feel great.

"Do you mind if I take a quick bath?" I asked.

"Oh, my hot water tank broke. It just happened."

"Oh." Confused, I looked at the change of clothes and toiletries I was holding.

"We'll go to the beach later and wash off." Cheryl said this without any concern as she served breakfast. "Come eat with us."

Throughout the years, whenever we came to the Island, along with the crazy fun I had, misadventures also ensued. These always slipped my mind until moments when things like no hot water and a dog running around with a dead chicken entered the scene.

Mark returned and appeared as confused as I did to find out there wasn't any hot water. We gobbled up breakfast and headed to the beach. Cheryl took Nicole and the children in her vehicle and Mark and I followed in our car. It gave us a chance to talk.

"Camper Henry looks drunk all the time," I said.

"Yeah."

"Your mom's friend Michael seems like a nice guy, but his dog killed that chicken."

"Those chickens!" Mark exhaled while shaking his head.

I nodded. "I know. Well, whatever. I guess we can put up with some chickens for a while." We both laughed a little.

We bought chips and pop for Mark and the kids, and red wine and Twizzlers for Cheryl, Nicole, and me. We tried our best to get clean at the beach and had some fun in the sun before heading back.

We pulled up and Camper Henry sauntered over to the car. A beer bottle in hand, he slurred his words a little. "Well, we buried the chicken. We have to keep Annabelle close. She is a little unpredictable," he chuckled and walked away.

That night Cheryl planned a large dinner that included our family and several of her friends. Mark complained to me that he wanted to keep the gathering small, but that wasn't Biker Nana's style. Trying to blend in, he put a smile on his face, and we helped prepare for a nice feast. Once everything was ready, we brought the food down.

I met everyone and was excited for a night of good music, drinks, and a delicious meal. We settled into our seats and started passing around the food when I noticed a wasp come up behind Erin who was sitting across from me. Concerned, I motioned to Erin; she turned her head and her face almost touched the wasp. She pushed her chair back and jumped up to avoid the menacing bug.

"Oh, is that a wasp?" Cheryl asked, "Ignore it."

Erin stared at me astonished at this request and shook her head.

Right then, four more wasps showed up to the party. *Here we go again.* I'm not sure why bees and wasps were so abundant on many of our trips, but I could swear they had it out for our family. Now all three kids jumped up as the wasps darted back and forth over the table and around all our heads.

"You have to ignore them," Cheryl said. "They'll go away."

We got the children back in their seats, but they stiffened their bodies as they tried to sit still. I didn't enjoy my meal or the following conversations as much as I should have as my concern shifted to watching the kids. Cheryl was right, though; for the most part, the wasps left us alone if we ignored them. It was a test of patience. So far, most of this trip was a test of patience.

We played Trivial Pursuit and then turned in. Tired, still dirty, and still craving a good sleep, we prepared for our outdoor bed. Same as the night before, I put my hood up leaving only enough room to breathe.

"Goodnight," I said. I heard Mark swat a mosquito.

"Goodnight," he replied, finding my mouth in the dark and giving me a kiss.

## DAY 4:

The chickens didn't wake me up. Mark opened their cage before their squawking started. I hadn't heard a thing. Instead, something much more menacing crept up on me. My nostrils flared in and out. I inhaled an unfamiliar morning odour. I sat straight up in bed. What was that smell? Smoke! I tore back the curtain and the morning air that had always promised the scent of spruce trees was filled with an assaulting burnt odour. The sky was a yellow haze.

Mark had already joined the others when I walked into the loft.

Reports had come in that several fires were burning on the Island and the air quality was severely affected. The lack of rain was dire. Our area was safe, but nonetheless, the smoke veiled the entire island.

Mark told me he had not slept well at all. The long drive to the Island and the lack of sleep were beginning to take its toll on him. He was moody and there didn't seem like much I could do to help him. As much as I hoped each visit here would be better, I now realized that we had reached a familiar turning point.

Mark's attitude was going downhill fast. He loved his mom, but he clashed with her on the day-to-day plans. The kids didn't listen as well to his instructions and took their cues from "fun Nana". This irritated him as they ignored his requests. Too much socializing and partying wasn't Mark's style. He only wanted to spend time with his family and his mom. But Cheryl always enjoyed the whirlwind of life, and her adventurous spirit conflicted with his agenda of getting away for a relaxing holiday.

Although Mark and I had the same mindset of how we wanted to spend our days while on vacation, I was a little more open to spontaneous ideas. This wasn't an innate trait of mine, but when on vacation and at the mercy of your host's ideas and wild friends, if you can't beat 'em, you gotta join 'em. I threw my hands up in the air and rolled with the craziness around me, or else I'd have been miserable, like Mark often was.

We were now annoyed with one another, which prompted me to insist he take some time for himself while the rest of us went to the beach. He did, which relieved some of the tension.

I sat on beach towels with Cheryl and Nicole while the kids splashed in the water. The smoky sky didn't bother any of them. They were good like that; they didn't let things like wildfires get in their way of fun. I followed suit and tried to enjoy myself. We stayed all afternoon.

As we arrived back at Cheryl's place, we could see something going on. Michael and Camper Henry were chasing Annabelle. Once again, she had a chicken carcass in her mouth. Camper Henry ran back and forth with arms outstretched trying to rein in the dog. "Annabelle!" he shouted. He glanced at us driving up. "She dug up the carcass!"

An hour or so later, Mark came back. Even though we had gone our separate ways during the day to try to reboot our communication, the breakdown between us happened again. Mark was fed up with the situation and I was fed up with Mark and his tense attitude. We focused on making dinner in the loft while everyone else sat outside having drinks. We didn't say much to one another. As we prepared the salad, I could hear angry shouts outside. We stopped what we were doing and listened.

"What is that?" I asked. We walked to the opened loft door.

"Oh no. That's Mom's psycho neighbour."

"That guy's still yelling at her? What about? She got rid of her dogs. I thought he only complained about the barking."

We listened at the door as Cheryl's boyfriend, Camper Henry, and her friend, Jack, stood on one side of the high fence that separated their property. The faceless, angry man yelled from the other side somewhere beyond the trees.

"You better get your camper off my property! I'm going to come over there with a gun!"

Jack's face flushed a red hue. "Then I'll get MY gun!"

I turned to Mark. "What? The neighbour is coming with a gun?"

"No. No, he's just crazy. He gets drunk and yells at Mom. He's been doing it for years."

"Just crazy? Well, that's great. We're sleeping outside with mosquitoes, and squawking chickens, and smoky toxic air, and now we have to worry about this screaming psycho coming over with his gun? Are you fucking kidding me?" I walked back towards the kitchen and poured myself a large glass of Surprise Wine. Mark tried to reassure me, but I wasn't having it.

After a few deep breaths, a few minutes, and a few sips, I decided it didn't help me to stay angry and I did my best to ignore all of it. We served dinner and the wasps made an appearance. I had to keep my hand over my wine glass; if they flew in there and I took a gulp, one could end up in my mouth.

By this point, the neighbour has stopped yelling, and everyone disbanded. Camper Henry said goodnight and stumbled off. Mark wanted me to come to bed but I decided to stay up with Nicole and sit on the deck drinking more wine. We talked and laughed and even though I was frustrated with the vacation, I didn't mention anything. I thought about how we just had a couple nights left after this. I decided to make the best of it. The wine flowed and Mark began to come check on me every half hour or so. He glanced at my large glass of wine, crossed his arms, and asked when I was coming to bed.

"Soon," I replied. "You know we're on vacation, right?"

'Soon' turned into another hour and when I got myself to bed, Mark was still awake and fuming. "I thought you were coming to bed? I waited up for you!"

"Well you didn't have to. I lost track of time. What's the big deal?" I was angry now.

Our argument went on for far too long and veered off into all sorts of directions. I started crying. I felt like I was losing my mind.

And then something happened that had never happened before. The thought of leaving came into my head. Not only leaving the Island. But leaving Mark. Leaving the kids. I didn't need to be a part of this craziness. Why was I even here? I remember telling Mark before crying myself to sleep, "This life. This whole thing I agreed to. It's turning me into an alcoholic."

I fell asleep thinking that I wanted to get out of there as soon as possible.

## DAY 5:

Mark got up once the chickens began making noise. This time I felt him crawl back into bed. He put his arm around me. Barely awake, I remembered the late night battle we had but sunk into the comfort of his arms, snuggling close against his chest. I opened my eyes just a little, and among the many tattoos on his arms, I saw the one of my nickname that he had inked on his inner bicep from a few years back: "Frankie Moon". He started calling me this when we lived provinces apart at the beginning of our new relationship, when we were missing one another desperately. "Frankie", as a play on one of my middle names, and "Moon" from a tale about a spirit named Kuekuatsu who was in love with the moon.

The story has it that Kuekuatsu was deceived by another jealous spirit named Trickster. Trickster wanted the moon for himself, so he convinced Kuekuatsu to go to Earth and pick wild roses to give to his love, the moon. Kuekuatsu didn't know that he would no longer be able to return to the spirit world. Now on Earth, he had to change form and became a wolf. He misses the moon and every night he looks up to her and howls her name, but he can never hold her again.

Mark didn't look like a romantic, but I knew he was. He brought me flowers and wrote me poems. He was a strong man and always made me feel protected and important. I softened as I exhaled deeper into him, remembering the love we shared and the life we had built together.

Right then I felt something jump on the bed at our feet. Mark and I sat straight up at the same time. I almost tore the hood off my head to see what it was. A large chicken had hopped on the bed.

"Squuuak!" It screamed as it clucked around the sheets.

We spun our heads towards each other in disbelief. I was tired, dirty, hungover, and now enraged.

"That is fucking it! I have had enough! We are either getting a hotel room tonight or we are breaking up!" I sobbed.

Mark brought me down an aspirin and a glass of water and got me out of there. Cheryl offered to keep the kids while we left, sensing things were not going well for us. We went for breakfast and talked. We took a long walk in the woods by our favourite waterfall. I didn't want to end our relationship, but I did need some things to change. He understood. I also *immediately* needed some peace, a shower, and a bedroom with four walls and no chickens.

We booked a room at an ocean-side resort that evening. We soothed our tense muscles in the outdoor hot tub, walked around the grounds admiring the quiet landscape, and enjoyed a long shower before crawling under crisp white sheets in a comfortable bed.

We turned the TV on to the news. We watched a story of a man who punched a cougar in the face to save his dog. With such dry conditions on the Island, cougars were having a hard time hunting, so they had started targeting humans and pets. It warned: residents should be careful. Put your small animals away, especially after dark. I glanced at Mark. "We are NOT sleeping beside those chickens again."

That concluded our holiday on the Island.

## SNAPSHOTS

*Erin and Curtis doing dishes talking with each
other while I'm not paying much attention*

Curtis: "I like when they put the vibrator in my mouth."

Me: "What did you say?"

Curtis: "At the dentist, I like when they put the vibrator in my mouth."

Me: "It's definitely NOT called a vibrator."

Curtis: "Oh, well, that's what I call it."

Me: "Not anymore."

# Chapter 24

# HEARTSTRINGS

I heard the roaring muffler a block away. I stood up from the cement steps in front of my mom's front door and walked to the sidewalk knowing I would see her car at any moment. She pulled up in her silver El Camino. Leaning over and looking at me through the open passenger window, she tilted her sunglasses down. My sister Jennifer's black hair had grown quite a bit since I last saw her.

"Hey, Bean," I greeted her with the nickname that my two other siblings and I had given her when we were younger.

I was visiting Winnipeg. At least twice a year I came back to reconnect with my family and friends who lived there. I was especially excited to get away this time. Curtis and Erin had developed an endless pattern of nagging one another. Their escalating voices travelled up through our floors and screaming arguments broke out daily. It was wearing on my frayed nerves. I told them, "One day when you're all grown up, you can decide you never want to talk again! But right now, you have to live together. You need to try to get along."

Jennifer and I rarely talked these days. But we did send each other the odd text message. I asked her for gardening tips and she sent me something ambiguous every few months around 2:00 a.m. in the morning. Last month was a clip from her favourite 1980's sitcom, *The Golden Girls*.

She revved the engine. A cigarette dangled from her lips. She gave me a cunning grin, "Jump in." It sounded like a dare.

Having dabbled in all sorts of smoking since age thirteen, my sister had become a professional in her early forties; she needed no hands to puff away as we took off. The smell of empty beer bottles rose from under her driver's seat. I didn't see them, but I knew they were there from the night before, or maybe from this morning.

"Nice wheel cover," I said.

She gripped the leopard print. "Oh yeah? You like it? What do you think of my fuzzy dice?"

Two oversized black and white dice hung from the rearview mirror and as the car rumbled down the road, they danced joyously like guests at a party. And they *were* at a party of sorts. Jennifer's life was a string of one thrill-seeking event to the next. Going anywhere with her was always a nail-biter.

"How long are you in town for?" she asked.

"A week."

"Are you going to come out to see my little chickies?"

She lived on an acreage a couple of hours north of the city and spent most of her days gardening and tending to her boyfriend's dogs, Jimmy and Santo. Though her real love was swooning over her baby chickens.

One time, someone left the door open to the little barn on a hot summer day. Santo massacred the lot of them. She was heartbroken, and never forgave him. Luckily, her boyfriend warmed her heart back up by bringing in a new batch of cute yellow chicks.

While in the garden pulling weeds, Jennifer was also able to enjoy her habit of smoking weed. A life of growing romaine lettuce and horseradish while puffing on a joint left her quite content. When the day was done and she had washed the dirt from her hands, she was able to relax. She jumped into bed, grabbed a beer out of the mini fridge that was within arm's length, and watched a movie.

"Does Dad know when we're picking him up?" she asked.

"You were late, so I told him I'd call and let him know when we were a few minutes away."

She was always late, so there was no surprise there. I thought it was important to point it out every time anyway. To her credit, she was the only one who agreed to go visit Dad with me. I took what I could get.

We pulled up in front of his building where he sat on a bench with his friends, smoking and waiting for us to arrive. Once we got out of the car, a small smile surfaced as he walked over to us, arms outstretched. He always walked slowly. The steady stream of medication he took for his schizophrenia seemed to slow all his movements and at times, his thinking. A cigarette hung from his mouth. He squinted as some smoke irritated his eyes: not quite the professional smoker his middle daughter was.

"Did you hear me coming, Dad?" Jennifer asked as she hugged him.

"No," he said. His hearing wasn't as good as it had once been. He looked at her car. "That thing is a beast."

Dad wore old wrinkled clothing and smelled musty, like he had not showered in days. And he probably hadn't. He wore Vogue dark rimmed eye glasses that clashed with his dollar store watch. When I had asked him how come he had such expensive eyewear, he responded that the woman at the glasses store said they looked good on him and that he could get a senior's discount.

"Where do you want to go eat, Dad?" I asked while hugging him, leaning my face as far away from his Export "A" as possible.

"McDonald's is fine."

Of course it was. For years, I had pleaded with my dad to embrace more out of life; I offered to take him to nice restaurants, brought him shower products, and asked if he wanted new bedding. 'No, it's fine. Don't bother,' was the answer to my efforts. He either refused or gave away anything we bought him, but my siblings and I knew he always accepted a small bottle of whisky, or an occasional outing to get a burger.

It was obvious to me that he had a hard time looking after himself. But I was tired of rambling off solutions to problems that he ignored. Among many things, his hygiene needed improvement, as well as his diet. But he never complained about any of it, even the chronic infestation of bed bugs in the apartment block he lived in. He seemed to accept his life the way it was. I decided it was easier to bite my tongue and nod my head instead of expecting him to change. A burger he wanted, a burger he would get. Maybe an ice cream cone to follow.

We crammed into the front of the two-seater grey beast. Before Dad could get his seatbelt hooked up, Jennifer peeled away.

We settled in with our trays at a table in the middle of the busy restaurant. Small children chased one another while their parents tried to reign them in with promises of dessert if they stayed seated.

While my father ate his fries, Jennifer had a range of stories about the cast of characters in her small town. "There were too many beavers, Dad. So, they put a bounty worth fifty dollars for every tail we brought them. I went with Billy J and Uncle Ralph to set traps. The suckers were gone from the ditches, so it was something to do that summer."

I didn't understand what she was talking about half of the time. Her anecdotes were mostly random. Dad nodded as he continued chewing his food, raising his eyebrows to show interest. I always noticed how he laughed quite a bit when she talked.

She switched from hunting beavers to the cat cemetery behind her old shed where she put up small wooden crosses made of popsicle sticks over their graves. "The coyotes got them when they strayed too far from home." Her favourite cat, Lucky, hadn't been so lucky in the end either and was buried behind the shed too.

As more stories came flying out of her mouth, she relayed her adventures, often rising up out of her chair to act it out as a short play to entertain us. I couldn't help but fall under her animated spell, and I laughed. I shook my head at the reality she lived in. It was like she was from a different world. Loud and uninhibited, her raspy voice filled the restaurant. Her vocal cords sounded baked from all the tar she had inhaled for so many years. Strangely, her hallmark giggle was like a little girl. It was always shy as she covered her mouth.

The rest of the visit, I listened as she and my dad lapsed in and out of speaking French as they often did. Jennifer had lived with our dad throughout most of her teen years, allowing her to keep up her conversational French. I had lost the fluency of *le langage de l'amour* over the years while living full time with my mom. Mom was Hungarian and fluent in her own language, but it was never taught to any of us.

I always believed Jennifer was my dad's favourite and it never bothered me. They seemed to share a much stronger father-daughter bond. I teased her about it sometimes, which I think she liked. Maybe their connection was stronger because they never judged each other. I couldn't help but think that both of them could put some effort into improving the quality of their lives.

It was still sunny and hot when she dropped me off. I breathed a sigh of relief that I was returned in one piece.

"I'll call later, and we'll make plans for you to come out to my place," she said.

I nodded, unsure if I would go or not. I never knew how to feel after spending time with her. If we weren't sisters, would we choose to be in each other's lives?

I thought about what I had told Curtis and Erin: "One day when you're all grown up, you can decide, and you never have to talk again if you don't want to." But as I stood there watching her light up her cigarette before leaving, that statement didn't feel true.

I felt my heartstrings, linked to hers. Intertwined with ribbons of DNA and memories, they swirled in my chest. As she drove away, I felt a tug as the invisible strands between us stretched. They snapped. As connected as we were, we were just as disconnected. We no longer shared a bunk bed and blueberry bushes. Years had passed and the different worlds we had created left me in a place where I didn't quite know her anymore. The El Camino turned the corner and once again my sister was gone, disappearing like smoke.

# Chapter 25
# MOM

It was October and I was ten years old when I was transferred out of our small town school to be registered in a city elementary class. It was the year we moved into The Chicken Coop. That's what my mom called our new one-bedroom home on Pilgrim Avenue. After leaving my dad she rented a place in Winnipeg: a tiny suite upstairs in a house and the only place she could afford in a decent neighbourhood.

My two oldest siblings had moved into adulthood and were fending for themselves, so my mom, Jennifer, and our grey cat Herman squeezed into The Chicken Coop.

Our new home was cozy enough, but someone, probably the previous tenants, had used a black marker to draw a huge Harley Davidson logo on the slanted ceiling in our living room. Andy, the guy who lived on the main floor and owned the home, hadn't re-painted before we moved in.

A few small windows brought in the day's sunbeams for a short time during the autumn that we moved in. I was used to large living room windows, a large yard, and privacy. I imagined my cat missed it as much as I did. The houses in the city were so close together and I could see into our neighbours' kitchens as I walked by.

I began walking fifteen minutes to and from school instead of taking a school bus. Robyne, who became my best friend, lived two streets down from me on Stranmillis Avenue. Although we were in different grade four classrooms, we began skipping home together after school. Eventually, she started doubling me on the back of her blue ten-speed bike. It took another year before my mom could afford to buy me my own.

I caught the chickenpox the summer after we moved in. The amount of heat and humidity that rose up and collected in the second floor of The Chicken Coop weighed thick in the air. Being unable to leave the suite for ten days while scratching and dabbing calamine lotion on my skin was a struggle. The order not to scratch the inflamed blisters and the patches of dried white dots all over my body wasn't what was most upsetting. The worst part was being stuck in The Chicken Coop on those smoldering days.

Robyne and I were joined at the hip. If we weren't delivering flyers during the week, she and I went door to door asking if we could rake the owner's lawn for four dollars. We supplied the rakes, they had to supply the bags. I can only imagine what we looked like: two skinny blonde-haired girls, standing there with rakes taller than us. But people agreed to hire us. This kept us busy earning money and allowed us to go to arcades or get excited when we heard the Dickie Dee melodic bells coming a block away.

Dickie Dee was an ice cream company that was founded in Winnipeg in 1959. Employees, who were always teenagers in my neighbourhood, rode a modified tricycle that had a large boxy compartment on the front that held many different flavours of popsicles and ice cream. Children came running out of their houses from all over chasing down the Dickie Dee bike that regularly road up and down the streets during the hot summer months. At that age, we could barely find our house key or library books, but you can bet we tracked down the bells that jingled on the front of the Dickie Dee bike!

Andy, from downstairs, often called Jennifer and me to wash and dry his dirty dishes. Instead of washing them himself, he hid them away under his sink until he ran out of clean ones. We earned a few bucks there, too. If the Dickie Dee wasn't around, the corner store had an array of candy, and the owners were happy to take our money.

Despite all that, we were happy there. I never had to wake up to the heavy and aggressive voice of my dad again.

Even though The Chicken Coop took most of my mom's paycheck, she had enough to buy an old red Chevy Nova. She also saved a little to buy herself some new clothing and lipstick. My mom had always enjoyed taking her time to apply make-up. Before then, she had only worn it on a rare date night with my dad or on special occasions. On their nights out, I remember the babysitter settling in and the scent of my mom's lipstick on my cheek when she kissed us goodbye.

But now, she applied makeup every morning. She also wore a trendy new full-length red coat and long-brimmed hat to match. It was the 80's and bright colours, distinct eyeliner, and Fire Engine Red lipstick were in. With her shoulder-length brown curls and hazel eyes, thin frame and long legs, she was a knockout. Add in high heels and Chanel No. 5 and the men turned their heads.

There was no shortage of suitors waiting for a chance to take my mom on a date. I knew this because I often answered our black rotary phone and heard a male voice asking for my mother. Our tiny home had no space for private conversations.

Even though it was her nature to be coy, I think my mom enjoyed being *seen* for the first time in a long time. Feeling attractive, feeling confident. Not unlike the Party Moms.

But this Lady in Red was picky. For a few years she didn't have any serious interest in dating. Instead she hung around with Terry: a graphic artist she met through work who she always suspected was gay, though he never revealed this. Terry often met her for coffee at a place called Cousins Deli and Lounge, where many artists sat and talked for hours. An average-sized man with brown hair and a beard, he seemed to be a bit of a modern hippy. There was something eccentric about him, perhaps the way many true artists exude a 'je ne sais quoi'. My mom rarely drank alcohol and never smoked so they met to have cappuccinos. This took my mom away for the night. After applying her lipstick, the familiar scent of 'goodbye' kissed my cheek.

Robyne and I spent most of our time playing in the snow during the winters, or riding bikes and swimming at the community outdoor pool behind the Superstore in the summer. We got flashed by a pervert once while exploring a secluded bike trail; after jumping on our ten-speeds and peddling like hell to get out of the area, we had to tell the police all the details. "Penis" was not an easy word to say out loud when you were eleven years old. Through some ups and downs, my life was fairly simple when we lived on Pilgrim Avenue.

I imagine my mom's life was not simple. My mom never failed to wake early for her full-time job, turning on the radio to rouse us out of bed for school. She also never failed to provide a healthy dinner. I'm sure the Lady in Red had other interests, but she dutifully gathered the dirty laundry and loaded my sister and me into the Nova to spend a Saturday at the laundromat when it was needed. She never complained.

I was now the same age that my mom was all those years ago when we lived in The Chicken Coop. But I complained all the time.

*****

My mom had re-married a few years after divorcing my father, when I was around fifteen years old. My stepdad passed away a few months before Erin came to live with Mark and me. My mom now lived alone in the house that she and I had moved into, along with her new husband all those years ago.

She found that many women in her life were becoming widows. With their sudden freedom and making efforts to embrace a different lifestyle, they talked about travel and were preparing for future adventures.

I was still visiting friends and family in Winnipeg. I had spent time with Jennifer and my dad at McDonald's the day before, now I was spending time with my mom.

"I don't think it's so bad." I held the small black and white picture close to my face.

"Are you kidding? It doesn't even look like me," my mom laughed, "After the woman handed me the pictures, I burst out laughing right there in front of her. She looked at me like I was nuts!"

"It's only a passport photo. No one really sees it anyway," I assured her.

She was right, though. It was a funny photo because the serious older woman in the picture staring back at me didn't look like my mom.

I knew it wasn't accurate, but I had a way of keeping my mom young in my mind: full makeup, dark hair, high heels. My memory had locked in these images of her from a different time, when my life moved slower, and when I watched her more. Seeing pictures of her now, thirty years older, glasses, grey shoulder length hair, challenged my reality of her. *She couldn't truly be this age.* Maybe I would always envision my mom as the Lady in Red, but in some ways she was unmistakably the quirky senior that sat across from me.

"Mom, they don't have your middle name right. It says 'Alice' here. Didn't you notice?"

"Yes, that is my middle name."

"I thought it was Olga?" I was confused.

"Apparently not."

"What do you mean, 'apparently not'"?

"Well, I guess it was a religious name that my parents gave me, but it wasn't official," she shrugged.

"Are you serious? You're telling me that at nearly seventy years old, you're only now finding out your real name?"

"Yeah."

Even though I thought it was odd, it didn't seem to faze her.

My mom always had stories when I was visiting. They were funny, but she didn't know they were funny. A few years back, she told me about a road trip with her sister, when they drove down south across the border to do some shopping in the United States. After buying a few items, in the booming metropolis of *Grand Forks*, they opened the trunk to put their bags in. It was only then that they saw the dirty, bloody bags of knives and rags from my stepdad's latest hunting excursion. The two senior women wondered what they should do. They took a chance driving back. "Luckily the border patrol didn't ask to examine the car. It all worked out fine."

Another habit she had was buying and returning fruit, and telling me all the details. I have never known anyone else to return so much fruit, or any fruit for that matter. I always thought of fruit as a gamble when it's purchased. Not my mother. She takes a bite of something she doesn't like, and back it goes to customer service. I imagine the long-term employees probably know her name by heart, since she has lived in the same neighbourhood and shopped at the same grocery store for over twenty-five years. They must sigh when they see her coming with her bag of cherries in one hand and the sales receipt in the other.

"So, your middle name is 'Alice' then?"

"Yep. Do you want me to run and get you a coffee?" She knew I enjoyed a stronger brew than what she made. I was lucky she seemed to enjoy fussing over me when I was there and I wasn't resisting it.

While I waited for her to return, I stayed seated, wrapped in my old baby blue housecoat, adjusting the La-Z-Boy my stepdad used to sit in. The large windows allowed the morning sun to stream into the small sunroom. I watched tiny flecks of dust float in the bright beams. My eyes refocused. Beyond the flecks sat a large TV. My mom preferred it on; it filled her quiet time. I kept it off. I *needed* quiet time. I sat in front of it, at eye level, less than two metres away. I could see myself in the grey reflection of the screen. It was as though a stranger stared back at me. Unsmiling. Old. Numb. I looked away.

It had been a couple of years since we watched my stepdad pass away from heart disease. Now my mom lived alone in the house with her obese and spoiled cat. I had no connection to this animal. The chocolate-black oversized feline lay on the carpet mulling me over, moving nothing but the tip of her tail. I was in the fat cat's home now and she saw the same stranger in me that I saw in the TV screen.

Living two provinces away was tough at times. Mark and I had had all three kids for over a year. Not one of my family members or my friends from here had met them.

When I came back to visit, I stayed in my old bedroom. It felt like my life with Mark, Curtis, Erin, and James ceased to exist during my time here. My old robe hung behind the door of my teenage room, as though it waited for my visits. My former closet still housed items that didn't make sense to bring with me to my new life with Mark when I moved to Alberta. Yet, they were things that I wasn't ready to throw out. The closet held old pictures that sat in a shoe box, posters I had bought over the years, rolled and elasticized, laid in the corners. University text books I paid for handsomely were still stacked on the shelf above the hangers. The room sat untouched in many ways, like a museum of my former life. Holding some comfort and some confusion every time I visited and unpacked my luggage.

Ten minutes later my mom returned with the coffee. As she handed me the cup, I noticed a bunch of sugar packets in her other hand.

"I don't need extra sugar, Mom."

"Oh I know. I bring them for Auntie Lucy. She sometimes has coffee with me."

"But you own a sugar bowl, and it has sugar in it."

"Yes, but what happens is she dips her spoon in her coffee, then she dips her spoon back into the sugar bowl."

"And?"

"And the liquid clumps up the sugar and then makes everything sticky on the bottom."

"Oh. Ask her not to do that."

"No, no. I get these packets and ask her to use them. It's no big deal. I take them where I can find them."

"So, you steal packets of sugar wherever you go?"

"Yes."

She opened the cupboard and took out a bowl of sugar packets. All types from all sorts of restaurants. "See, I have a bunch of them."

"Jesus, Mom. You're like a squirrel, running around gathering and stashing nuts."

"Oh, it's no big deal."

"You're hilarious, Mom," I let out a little laugh while I sipped my coffee.

The following morning after coming back with my coffee, she went into great detail about how an older woman sitting at the restaurant was watching her as she was trying to make off with some packs of sugar. She pulled the packets from her pockets. "I had to hide what I was doing. I didn't want to get busted."

"Mom, you're going to get in trouble one day."

The next day we set out early for a drive to one of our most indulgent destinations. Grand Beach was located north of Winnipeg and hugged the eastern shore of Lake Winnipeg: Canada's sixth largest lake. The drive took about an hour and a half and was easily worth it. Among the sea of "Friendly Manitoba" printed licence plates, you were sure to see many out of province ones as well as tourists bustled along to this beautiful attraction.

My mom and I always preferred to roll down the windows and have the wind fly through our hair. She could be so carefree. Our breezy highway ride promised to lead to a day lazing around on the fine white sand, laying on beach towels with the sun warming our bodies, and cooling off in the shade on the grass-topped dunes when we got too hot. Even when the beach was crowded, you could find a quiet spot if you walked far enough as the beach spanned a length of three kilometres. We grabbed our beach bags and jumped in the car.

Before getting on the highway, we approached the drive-thru of a chain coffee place for my morning cup, I asked if my mom wanted anything. I told her I wasn't going to ask for extra sugar.

I leaned in to the speaker a little, "Can I get a medium coffee, double double, please?"

As I drove ahead my mom stared at me in disbelief, "Why didn't you ask for a 'Senior's coffee'?"

"Because I'm not a senior."

"But you would have saved fifty cents. I can't believe you didn't say 'Senior.'"

"Sorry, Mom. I guess lying to save fifty cents doesn't come naturally to me."

"It adds up over time! You better say 'Senior' next time. I can't believe you didn't say it!"

Towards the end of the week we went to one of our favourite restaurants and sat on the patio for a glass of wine and some dessert. In the center of the table was the standard small ceramic container of white sugar, brown sugar, and some other concoctions of aspartame, sucralose, and saccharine.

Her eyes lit up when we sat down. "Jackpot!" she said as she adjusted her yellow sun visor.

"No, Mom. This is a nicer restaurant. I don't want you stealing from here."

While I was talking, her hands were already reaching towards the sugar bowl. She shoved the packets into her black fanny pack like a professional.

As she was finishing up her five-finger discount, the waitress brought our menus. She hadn't seen anything. After telling us about the specials, I ordered a glass of wine.

She turned to my mom. "Would you like a glass as well?"

"Um, no," Mom's eyes surveyed the menu, "I'll have something else."

"We have coffee," she said, glancing at the sugar bowl. A moment of hesitation came upon her face. "That's funny. I could have sworn I filled up that sugar bowl before you sat down."

My eyes made their way to my mom who was still perusing the menu. With impeccable poise she raised her head and looked at the waitress. "I'll have a slice of the lemon cake, please. It's gluten free, right?"

The waitress took the menu from my mother while glancing back at the sugar bowl with lingering puzzlement.

"It is." She said as she walked off.

"Mom. You've got a problem."

# SNAPSHOTS

*James doing homework at the table*

Me walking by: "Why does your face look weird?"

James: "Because I'm holding in all my farts."

Me: "Oh."

*Walking by James five minutes later*

"James, you stink."

James: "That's because I let out all my farts when you walked by!"

# Chapter 26
# VOMIT

Curtis arrived home late on Sunday afternoon. He was twelve years old now and we were allowing him some freedom to go out on his own. He spent the day with his friend Colby.

When the two of them got together, they liked to eat junk food. This day, it was McDonald's. Curtis knew I didn't appreciate him gorging on fast food, especially before dinner, but this didn't stop him from filling me in on all the dirty details when he got home. It seemed he blew all of his allowance right then and there on as much food as his ten bucks would buy. He laughed while rubbing his protruding belly, proud of all the calories he'd consumed.

Later that night Curtis walked into the living room where Mark and I sat, now rubbing his stomach from discomfort. Like any parent, we were skeptical and told him to go lay down and relax.

Mark and I reminisced about times when we lied to our parents about "feeling sick" so that we'd have a chance to ditch school the next day. We both nodded with a smirk. Young Curtis was no match for us.

A few hours went by with Curtis walking past us at regular intervals, grumbling. Finally, I said, "Go to bed. I'm sure you'll feel better tomorrow."

He walked back downstairs to his room, continuing to moan and groan.

As Mark and I were about to head to bed ourselves, James came running up. "Curtis is puking!"

I froze. *Oh no. Anything but vomit.*

I used to know this kid named Jeffrey from our neighbourhood. We were all around thirteen years old. He had long, dirty blond hair, wore a leather jacket, and spoke very softly. We went to his place sometimes and listened to Aerosmith for hours. I don't know what happened to his mom and dad, but he was being raised by his grandparents. He was a nice kid, but lonely, I think.

One night, he and a few other guys I went to Junior High school with, drank way too much Jack Daniels and came knocking on the basement apartment window where I lived with my mom. When I went outside to say hi, Jeffrey keeled over on the cement stairs outside the door and began throwing up. My mom came out and saw what was happening. She decided to call the police to help him. They called an ambulance to take him to the hospital and pump his stomach. The next day he told us, in his soft voice, that it sucked.

The other time we had a vomit episode to contend with was when Mark and I were on Vancouver Island a few years back. It was Christmas time and we were visiting the kids. We decided to have breakfast at Denny's restaurant. Biker Nana met up with us and when we were distracted by the menu, she ordered James a chocolate milkshake, which he gulped down in a couple of minutes. The food came and while we ate, I noticed James sucking up a second chocolate milkshake, care of Biker Nana once again. Two milkshakes back to back. About a minute after finishing the second one he threw it all up. Mark ushered a wobbly and sick James to the bathroom to clean him up. I sat stunned, not knowing where to even begin with this situation. I was not capable of cleaning up this mess. The bald fat guy in sweatpants in the booth across from us looked at me like I was the worst mom in the world. It was only my third visit to the Island with the kids; they barely knew my name. I wanted to convey that in my eyes to the large man, but that's not a look I know how to relay without words.

The waitress came up to the table with some cleaning accessories while shaking her head and said, "Just go." We left her a huge tip and got the hell out of there, fast.

Now Curtis was throwing up and I was no longer just their dad's girlfriend or the thirteen-year-old girl looking to my mom for guidance. Now I was the mom. A wave of pride hit me: I was coming to Curtis' rescue.

Mark and I rushed downstairs. Curtis was sprawled out on the floor outside the bathroom door, which was shut, moaning in pain while clutching his gut.

"Curtis? Are you okay?" I was concerned. I had never seen Curtis ill like this before. I helped him into his bed and told him I would get a cold cloth for his head. "It was the McDonald's!" He bellowed almost incoherently.

Mark opened the bathroom door and was staring in. His face stationary and unflinching. The smell yanked my nose and I turned my gaze to inside the door as well. There was vomit everywhere. I'm not sure how it reached all four walls and not the inside of the toilet.

I ran upstairs and grabbed a roll of paper towels. I peeled off sheets to clean up.

"I can clean it," Mark said.

"No, no, I can help," I replied.

The minute I began trying to scoop the mess, I began gagging. I gave my head a shake and reset my thoughts. *You can do this.* I stuck my nose into my shirt to avoid the smell, but the visual of this catastrophe began to make me dizzy. *Do we own goggles and a nose plug?* My heart beat faster and I continued to gag. It was too much. A strong wave of nausea hit me. I stopped and stood up, "I'm going to throw up!"

"Go upstairs," Mark waved me off.

I bolted to the front door and stuck my head outside into the cold fall air, gasping, nearly hyperventilating. I slowed my breathing, sat down on the couch, and waited for Mark. I felt terrible. I had abandoned him in the trenches.

It was some time before he returned upstairs. He calmly washed his hands and sat down next to me on the couch.

"It was everywhere. How could he have gotten it everywhere but in the toilet?" He said.

I don't know how long we sat there in numbed silence, but it was a while.

# SNAPSHOTS

*Conversation with Mark, getting ready for bed*

Me: "It's cold in the mornings now. When you get out of bed, can you throw this extra blanket on me? Otherwise I wake up cold and I find it hard to warm up during the day. It totally makes me miserable."

Mark: "Okay, I'll try to remember."

Me: "Deal?"

Mark: "No, not "deal"; I said I'd try to remember."

Me: "Okay. Can you please throw the extra blanket on me or I will wake up cold and miserable and probably not be "in the mood" until I warm up, which will be next summer."

Mark: "Deal."

# Chapter 27

# 5 À 7

'Cinq à sept' is a French term that means: 'Five to Seven'; as in the time 5:00 p.m. to 7:00 p.m. In France, this phrase originally implied a time when an illicit sexual rendezvous could potentially take place. Holding an affair during these hours provided convincing excuses: working late, running errands, or being stuck in traffic—a time when it was easier to slip away unnoticed.

I never had an affair, but I did cherish these hours for a different reason. Before living with the kids, I spent the hours from five to seven much differently. Strolling home after work, which used to be within walking distance, I entered the peace and quiet of our one-bedroom apartment. Living up on the third floor made it easy for me to climb out of my work clothing and walk around in my intimate attire if I so desired.

Mark arrived afterwards and following a gentle kiss hello we sat on the couch and talked about our day. Most days, we made a fancy little dinner for two. Or, if we didn't feel like cooking, we prepared a snack. When experiencing an especially tiring week, maybe we'd take a nap on the couch, falling asleep in each other's arms. We could watch The Food Network on

TV, listen to Sam Cooke's greatest hits, or go for a walk. I relied on Cinq à Sept as a welcomed catalyst between day and night.

I had not seen the sunlight in days. The long cold January hours of early darkness gave way to a late morning of dull clouds. Day after day they blanketed the city. I held my breath waiting for a crack of colour from the sky. *Does the sun still exist?*

Mother Nature would not be rushed after providing the Winter Solstice on December 21$^{st}$. She still saw fit to keep my patience in check, feeding me one or two extra measly minutes a day, and somber ones at that. My soul ached for the light and heat of summer.

I stood gazing out the front window of the herbal apothecary where I worked. Under the streetlamps, the fluffy snowflakes swayed in the air as they floated to the ground and were beginning to glow in contrast to the darkening afternoon sky.

I was cozy inside. Our essential oil diffusers emitted a delicate misting of water in the air creating a peaceful ambience. Our section had unique niche items for sale: an assortment of high-end herbal teas with no artificial flavours, beeswax candles, and a huge selection of organic oils. Dozens of plants decorated the shelves and floor, giving a warm welcome to customers as they entered.

"Ohhhh…what's that lovely smell?" many would ask while we handed them a sample of warm Spiced Plum tea.

"It's just the scent of our store," we would reply with a smile.

But today, the customers were a little frazzled. The snow wasn't tapering off. It looked lovely moving in the breeze, but it was accumulating into a slippery mess on the streets. After a few shoppers mentioned several car accidents they had seen during the day, I decided to leave work at 4:30.

I brushed the snow off my car windows and jumped in, hoping to beat some of the rush hour traffic. I backed up fast to get through the mounds behind my wheels and slammed right into the telephone pole that I parked beside every morning. The one small area of the back window that I failed to clear hid the pole from my view.

I got out and assessed the damage. *Fuck. How stupid.* I wasn't hurt, but the bumper and taillight weren't so lucky. Now I had one more thing to add to the list of things to take care of. The list never ended.

I joined the slow-moving traffic and turned the radio on to a classical station. I reached my hand around to my upper back and gave it a little rub to relieve some stiffness.

When the gusty winds of winter hit me in November, a deep freeze burrowed into my spine. It forced my shoulders up in a semi-permanent position of tension. The uncomfortable chill I felt was a little worse with each passing day. I slept with heating pads, wore thick scarves, and lived in turtlenecks hoping to combat it. There was no winning. As the season wore on, the cold radiated out from my spine and into my nerves. Weeks went by trying to endure a shiver I could not shake off. What had presented in physical form, became a chronic problem that seeped into my personality. Mark was left with a frigid wife and the kids with an icy stepmother. A long hot shower seemed to be the only thing that could thaw me out.

The traffic continued as I crawled along with it. The congestion on the streets wasn't what bothered me. For months now, the depression descended upon me the closer I drove to our home. Just like the cold, the winter's darkness wasn't only measurable outside. It became palpable within me.

I was hungry and miserable. The last thing I felt like doing was cooking a meal and sitting down to eat with everyone. In the distance I saw the McDonald's golden arches illuminating the sky.

*Fuck it.* I turned the wheel and found myself in line at the drive-thru. I ordered a large fries and a cheeseburger: the same thing I used to order as a child on the odd occasion my parents would bring me to a fast food restaurant. Familiar, fun food. I placed the sack on the seat next to me. Once back on the road I didn't waste a moment. I nearly ripped open the small brown bag. The aroma wafted out and I inhaled. My fingers fumbled around looking for the fries. I crammed a handful in my mouth all at once like a gluttonous participant in a food eating contest. They were fresh and hot, but the burning in my mouth didn't stop me. I needed to feel anything but what I was feeling. My cheeks were stuffed like a chipmunk as I chewed. I was trying to swallow my sadness, resentment, and confusion with the food. Maybe it was working? *"Bah-da-bum-bah-bah! I'm Lovin'it!"*

I threw the last few in my mouth before activating our garage door opener and pulling in. It was 6:00 p.m. when I finally arrived home. The garage was pitch black, except for my headlights. There used to be a light that activated when we drove in. It began cutting out months ago until it refused to work at all.

I shut off the car and stayed seated in the dark. I glanced up through the garage window and could see Mark in the house. He stood in the kitchen, head down, maybe preparing food, or reading an article on his phone.

I hated walking in to see all the chores that awaited me; the dishes needed to be washed, the garbage needed to be taken out, school forms needed to be read and signed, or that one of us needed to run back out to the store to get bread or milk.

Arriving home felt like a second job, one that was all consuming between cinq à sept. I now despised this time of day. I remembered the old Tom Cochrane song, "Life is a Highway." These days, life felt more like a driveway.

I flashed back to the outing that Mark and I had with his sister's four daughters at an outdoor amusement park. It was a couple of years before we had the kids living with us. I excused myself to go find the bathroom and once returning to the group I made a rookie mistake. I passed an ice cream stand and bought myself a cone. When I walked up licking the creamy treat, the girls' mouths fell open. They pointed at me while crying out, "I want one, too!" Mark sighed and shook his head. "Did you think you were just going to re-join us with an ice cream cone and no one would notice?"

"I didn't think of it." I replied, shrugging my shoulders.

I looked down at the fast food bag. I couldn't walk into the house with the one cheeseburger I bought.

"Did you bring some for us?" They were sure to chant.

I unwrapped the crinkly package and took a bite. *Sorry everyone, this burger's mine.*

I sat for a few minutes, hoping that my selfish feast in the car would change my attitude. It didn't. I still dreaded going inside. When I opened our back door, I heard the kids race up the stairs to greet and hug me. I began to cry. Mark cut them off and asked them to go back downstairs. He hugged me and through my sobs I told him I needed a warm shower.

# SNAPSHOTS

*Erin, Curtis, and me sitting at the table after supper*

Me: "Curtis, I have to ask you a question later."

Erin: "You're probably going to ask him if he has pubic hair."

*Curtis looking awkward and shifty eyed*

Me: "I most certainly was NOT going to ask Curtis if he has pubic hair. There are some things I never need to know. That's one of them."

Erin: "Everyone gets pubic hair! Except for the smallest man in the world. He doesn't have any."

Me: "How do you know? Did you actually read that somewhere?"

Erin: "No."

Me: "Is this conversation even happening right now?"

Erin: "Yes. Yes it is."

# Chapter 28

# BUBBLY

On an overcast spring morning, Mark and I took our car to the mechanic. They told us it would be a three-hour wait so we went to a nearby restaurant for breakfast. The walk was cool but it felt good to know the warm weather was on its way.

It was only ten o'clock, but after I finished breakfast, I indulged in a glass of wine anyway. "That'll be a nine-ounce, please." The first sip saturated my brain almost instantly. I tilted my head to one side and admired Mark's green eyes. We rarely went out alone anymore. In these moments, it felt like it was just the two of us again. Even amidst the hustle of the waitresses carrying hot pots of coffee, and through the smell of waffles and omelettes, I felt like we were on a romantic date.

As we chatted, I couldn't help but notice a man and woman being seated near us. The woman was in her late fifties and had a glorious and confident smile as she walked. It was as though she were as light as air. She made her way past our booth. Her clothing flowed from her body; the cream and beige coloured outfit was unassuming. Her earthy appearance didn't overshadow her radiance. Her hair was shoulder length, the colour of clover honey, with large flowing curls. Everything about her seemed effortless, like she was floating in a bubble. I felt her vibe and floated with her.

"I wish I had curly hair," I said to Mark.

"Why?" He sipped his coffee.

I shrugged. "I've always wanted curly hair. I think it would suit my personality more."

"What personality is that?"

"Bubbly!" I flashed him a full smile as I swirled my wine around.

"What? You think *you're* bubbly?"

"You don't think I'm bubbly?"

Mark let out a good laugh, "No. You hate people." He said it as a matter-of-fact.

My smile faded.

It felt like he punctured the bubble I was floating in and handed me a twenty-pound bag of quicksand. He was right. How long *had I* hated people?

"I think I used to be bubbly," I said with a frown. I wasn't even sure anymore.

Was I once carefree and light, like the woman with the loose honey curls?

Mark noticed me in deep thought. "When do you think you were bubbly?"

I shook my head and drowned my last bit of optimism with a final gulp of wine.

"Who knows."

# Chapter 29

# UNDER PRESSURE

Robyne had a healthy baby boy. The pregnancy had some complications and the C-section she experienced was frightening, but it was worth the struggle.

She repeated what most mothers said: "I didn't know it was going to be this hard. I don't know what the hell I'm doing, but I'm figuring it out as I go. I'm trying."

She didn't have time to shower, didn't have time to eat, and didn't even have time to sit alone for a bowel movement. "I had to hold him while I was taking a shit," she said while we drank coffee. She put her hands up in front of me, as if she was holding the baby. Luckily, shame seemed to be erased from new mothers that I spoke with. It became a game of survival and sanity. Mama bears had no time for anything frivolous to worry about.

In the past when I had gone on weekend getaways with the Party Moms, they walked around naked in the hotel room while getting ready. I changed my clothing in the corner. One of the moms told me that after two children and complete strangers poking and prodding her at the hospital, the self-consciousness over her naked body disappeared. She earned thick varicose veins on her legs and purple tiger stripes on the lower side of her torso and wore them without shame.

Robyne said, "I called up all the women in my life who had babies and apologized to them. I didn't realize the everyday struggle. That's what I told them. I said: 'I'm sorry. I *didn't* know how hard this is.'"

Months later, another visit with Robyne showed me that she was becoming underweight.

"I think I had a mini nervous breakdown," she revealed.

She went on to explain that it all became too much. She needed more help from her husband, and the well-intentioned advice and invitations from extended family put pressure on her. To stay in a rhythm, she put her son on a strict sleeping and eating schedule. She needed the predictability in her home to keep her sanity in check. But the schedule also interfered with family gatherings that she was expected to attend. She tried to make it clear to her family members: this schedule was how she needed to live right now. Hoping for support, she was surprised to find them ignoring her schedule and even seeming offended. It had become an issue.

I could not believe what I was hearing. I looked her straight in the eye and said, "Fuck everyone else. This is your baby and your husband and your home. If anyone else doesn't understand, then they can be upset all they want. If this schedule is keeping you balanced and happy, then stick to it. It won't be like this forever."

She appeared stunned but began nodding as I was talking. It seemed as though nobody had given her this opinion before. "Thank you," she said.

"You know what I saw in IKEA the other day?" I asked. "I saw a mom pushing her baby around in a cart. She had a tattoo on her upper arm of that cute singing frog from the Bugs Bunny cartoons. It was all faded. She looked half-dead. *She* looked faded. I imagined her being young and excited to get that frog tattooed on her. I imagined her happy and full of energy. I wondered if the girl who wanted the singing frog still existed in her. Moms have to take care of themselves."

Once I was back home with Mark, I told him the story. He rolled his eyes and said, "That's what you told her? When you have a baby, you can't stay at home all the time. You have to figure out ways to make it work when you go out. It can't all revolve around the baby's schedule."

My eyes grew wide. "Are you telling me that it's better for Robyne to feel like she's having a nervous breakdown because of expectations that are placed upon her and that she should try to accommodate her friends and family instead of attending to her own sanity? Are you serious?"

"No. What I'm saying is that they need to find a way to make it work for them, socially, and for the baby. It shouldn't be one or the other."

"Look, I get the gist of what you're saying, but I disagree with you. I think she needs time to get her rhythm, and if her mental health is suffering, then who knows what state her marriage will be in. Do you think the baby is better off with parents who are arguing because they're mentally and physically exhausted? Do you think it would be worth making everyone else happy around her, while she suffers through it?"

I was getting worked up and jumping to conclusions all over the place. I had never had a baby, but Mark had three, so I tried to take that into consideration. He and his ex-wife had a volatile marriage, though, which made me suspicious of his advice.

"I'm not going to argue with you. I just think she needs to be more flexible with the whole schedule."

"Well, I don't. I think it's none of anyone's business and that the family should work around her baby plan at this stage. Not forever, but while she's having trouble."

It ended there. This wasn't an argument Mark and I had to have. Neither one of us knew all of the facts, and it wasn't for either one of us to judge. But it seemed to point to parallel conflicts we had in our home. It was no surprise that I chose to defend being a homebody and dismissing the requests of extended family and friends for my own mental health. Mark wanted to accommodate the expectations of extended family. He wanted to take time to visit with them and allow the kids to connect with their grandparents, aunts, uncles, and cousins.

Rhythm, rest, recreation, ritual. When we first got the children, these sacred practices were compromised. It hit a nerve to imagine Robyne's slipping away as well.

# Chapter 30
## GROWING PAINS

Dr. Mandel guided us into his office. I used to shake his hand and chit chat about how he was doing to be polite, but the more often we saw him, the more we dropped the niceties and dove into the problems we were having.

Mark began by complaining that he didn't have enough time for everything he wanted to do. It was hard to get the hours needed to go to the gym, or to play ball hockey. I nodded and interjected that I also didn't have enough time. When was I supposed to find time to study my ongoing nutrition courses, or to have some time for myself to relax?

About thirty minutes in, our words became tangled and anxious. Whiny. I went on and on. There wasn't any time left, I repeated. I wanted my time. MY time.

Mark and I were so wrapped up in our complaints that we didn't notice Mandel's patience wearing thin. With a wave of his hands, he finally interrupted us. "Wait a second. Do you two even *want* these kids?"

Mark and I stopped, stunned.

"Yes, of course we want them," Mark replied. "We fought for them for years."

"Yes, I know. I know you fought for them. But do you *want* them?"

I was speechless. Nobody had ever asked this.

He motioned his hands in a circle. "You two are no longer single. You are now in the *Family* life cycle with the children. You need to *live* in the Family cycle now."

It hit me hard. I felt like he pushed me into a pool of cold water.

I was still thinking as though it was only me. When Mark and I were alone, I had a great deal of time and freedom. Why did I ever think I could still possess the same amount of time for myself now?

Mandel continued. "Look, if you two aren't balanced, the kids will have a difficult time. You don't need to have them in all sorts of activities. You can still make time for yourselves, but it's different now." His words woke me up.

Our hour was up. I got in the car and began crying. Mark held me.

"It's growing pains," I said. That was the truth. It hurt to give my time, it hurt to lose control, and it hurt to change and grow into something else. Of course, I was depressed. I was resisting this cycle of my life. I longed for the past. I had dug in my heels and refused to turn the corner.

As Mark drove, I looked out the window and thought about James. The other day we were shopping for new runners. At nine years old, his feet were too big to fit into the little kid's shoes that lit up, or that had comic characters and Velcro straps on them. I had to kneel down in the shoe aisle and break the news to him: he was too big now, too grown up. He'd never be able to fit into those little shoes again. He tried not to, but he cried. Even though he understood, he was gutted by this. I bought him a pair of shoes that he settled on. He sat in the backseat of the car, whimpering under his breath all the way home.

Gazing out on the silent car ride home with Mark, I watched the grey sky and rain tap against the window. I cried too. I felt like I understood how James felt. There was no going back.

Did I *want* the kids? I asked myself. I thought about Curtis and me dancing in the kitchen as we blended up pesto with fresh basil from our small garden. I remembered Erin, giggling and plugging her nose as Mark tossed her around the Mexican resort pool. And James, little James who sat on my lap any chance he got and asked me to carry him to bed.

I had a choice. I chose the kids. I chose this life. I chose Mark. And if I had to go back in time, I would choose them all over again.

# Chapter 31
# BETTER

The children accepted that they would always have a thing called 'Veggie Snack' after school, and larger-than-usual salads with their dinner. I accepted that they would run up to me in the grocery store holding boxes of Mac and Cheese, begging me to buy a couple.

They knew what my reply would be. Pretending to be offended by their request I screeched, "Are you kidding?" Then just loud enough for them to hear I followed with, "Crap Shitter? You *want* to eat *Crap Shitter*?" All three would keel over in laughter, glancing around to see if anyone else heard.

Somehow it never got old. It might be the best joke I've ever told in my life. I spent years in university and dreaming about the successes I would have, only to end up exaggerating my voice down a grocery aisle with a spectacular play on a pasta brand's words: "Whaaaat? Crap Shitter?"

Here I was, walking down a grocery aisle on an average Friday evening, feeling like I was on stage at a comedy show with three kids in the audience. Is this what my life had turned into? Apparently so.

Even though Kraft Dinner wasn't the healthiest food, they were adjusting to a new formula, removing their synthetic dyes and adding spices. We were all trying to be better.

As I threw those Mac and Cheese boxes in the cart, I smiled while watching the kids continue to giggle.

The boys were getting better, too. Their hygiene was still an issue, and we gave them constant reminders to brush their teeth, wash their hair, and clean their ears, but they had come a long way.

Curtis knew how to turn on his charm and sense of humour when he saw I was overwhelmed. He was always generous with his hugs and he never held back his love. With no problem embracing his inner nerdiness, he often walked around wearing an assortment of ridiculous hats with the confidence of the Emperor in his new clothes. Never shy of the stage, he played the lead role of Santa Claus in his grade six Christmas play. Talking with other parents makes me believe Curtis is a very typical kid.

We held James back a grade after he moved in with us and started school. In the documentation we received from his teachers on Vancouver Island, James had angry outbursts and was ostracized by his fellow students. Once he joined our family, James developed a heart of gold and had a cul-de-sac of friends in no time. What he lacked in academic standing he made up for in his genuine and kind personality. Without being asked, he always offered to share whatever he had with anyone around him. Sure, he could probably brush his teeth more. But I now preferred to focus on the milestones he had reached since living with Mark and me.

The boys are the boys, and part of me will never understand them the way I do Erin. Mark says he did a lot of the crazy things that they do, and Mark turned out pretty darn good, so I guess they'll be okay. I think we'll all keep getting better as we go.

# Chapter 32

# DAUGHTER

A couple more years moved on with many ups and downs. The kids were constantly growing at different paces, but I thought the most obvious changes were in Erin as she grew into her teen years.

On a bright summer Saturday afternoon, Mark and I went for a walk. We were almost out of sight when Erin sprung up from the neighbour's porch where she had been playing with the children on our block. She called out to us just in time; we stopped and turned around. She leapt off the porch and began running semi-awkwardly towards us. A mix between a half-run and half-hopping. Erin had a habit of running with her arms straight down and her hands in little fists, which I always thought was weird but endearing.

We watched as she moved towards us. It was obvious that her body had become curvy, especially the top half. The run/hop method she was using was no doubt accentuating this.

Mark bowed his head and stared as the ground, "Dear God. It's like watching an episode of Baywatch." She reached us with a big grin and asked where we were going.

"For a walk," I responded. "Erin, honey, you need to wear a shirt that covers this area a little more," I motioned to my chest area and then pointed to her low-cut V-neck t-shirt.

She stood before us with her unkempt chestnut hair and her beat-up runners.

"Why?" she cocked her head to one side.

"Because your breasts are going to pop out of your shirt."

"Oh," she glanced down, "Whoops. Okay!" she laughed and hopped back to the neighbour's porch.

Mark and I knew that Erin was growing into a woman, despite her preference for gooey slimy things and her Disney sheet set. It was the strange age a girl goes through where they're developing, but they don't know what to do with their bodies because their sexuality is so new.

Her body was beginning to have a mind of its own, or rather, two large breasts of its own, and they were walking into every room before she did. I wanted her to understand her changing body as she became older, and that no doubt, others—and to my chagrin and Mark's wrath—full grown men, would take notice. Even though I gave Erin freedom with her personal style, I did want to instill modesty at this age and throughout her life.

I sometimes imagined Mark trying to have these personal conversations with her that were necessary as the years moved on. It's not that I believe men can't have profound and nurturing talks with their daughters. Of course, there are single dads and same-sex male partners who must. But unless one has experienced a menstrual cycle, then I imagine it could be tough to talk about it in a non-textbook manner. Mark didn't want anything to do with these conversations and it was clear from the beginning of our relationship that Erin knew who to come to for womanly advice regarding the changes she was experiencing.

Conversations went into great depth about the differences between pads, tampons, and The DivaCup. I explained over and over that it was a great thing to get a period; it was nothing to be scared of and something to embrace as you matured. I was happy when she announced she had hers as the fear-based questioning about it stopped and she was able to feel relief that it was no longer a mystery.

Of course, there were many other topics that came up. We talked at length about what kind of deodorant would be best for her—something which I had to bring up since she seemed immune to the wicked armpit odor that she developed in grade six. She refused to use my homemade hippy version of deodorant so I gave up and found myself standing in the antiperspirant aisle that was flooded with every scent you could imagine. She sniffed tube after tube to find her perfect scent. Watermelon. Was the aluminum in this antiperspirant going to give her breast cancer? Parenting was a lot of guessing. She wouldn't use mine and I could smell her when she walked in the door, so watermelon it was. I shrugged as I handed my credit card to the cashier.

Regular bra shopping also became necessary. It seemed every few months she would tell me that she needed a size up. As a late bloomer and average woman myself, it never occurred to me that I would ever need to find bras of more substantial proportions. For years I had heard from well-rounded girlfriends about the struggle to find these elusive expensive bras. I always figured that was one problem I'd never have to worry about. Lo and behold, there I was with Erin searching for the perfect—larger— fit. Watermelon deodorant was one thing, watermelon-size bras was quite another.

Before Erin walked into the dressing room, I took a good look at her.

She wasn't the little girl with the Chucky nightmares anymore. I loved her and who she was becoming. Every day she was growing and turning more and more into my daughter. And every day, I was growing, and turning more into her mom.

# SNAPSHOTS

*Sitting at the kitchen table watching Mark fold laundry*

"Your mom's texting me... She bought a sailboat! Then there's something here about taking sailing lessons and living on it."

*Mark continuing to fold towels* "Well, of course."

"She sent a picture. Oh, it has a name!"

*Zooming in on the picture to read the side of the boat*

"It's called... 'Blow Me.'"

# Epilogue

The truth was, I never fell in love with my kids. But I *had* fallen in love with Mark all those years ago. That made me want to find a way for real love to exist between me and his children. Even though I wasn't *in love* with them, I did my best to always *show* them love: I nurtured them with good food. I watched silly movies with them. I let them tell me goofy jokes and I pretended to laugh.

Until one day, we were cooking meals *together*. They were asking me what movies *I* wanted to watch. They were telling me jokes that I didn't have to pretend were funny; I could laugh because over the years, we had started understanding each other's sense of humour.

I wish I would have known that loving my kids would take time. It never has to be love at first sight. My feelings for them grew by consistently showing up for them. My love for my youngest, James, was built by sitting on the floor with him, assembling Lego block after Lego block. With Erin, laughter created our love, during our girls' nights of wearing face-masks and applying nail polish. With Curtis, the recipe for love was by spending time in the kitchen, teaching him to cook family meals.

The kids accepted me with open arms from the beginning and even though I had a harder time acclimatizing to being a stepmom, I knew how special it was that they gave their love to me freely. I was so lucky. Now I can't imagine my life without them.

Something that helped us along, and that we still do now is "Our Gratefuls". This was something we began doing with the kids once we started having family dinners together. We each had to say three things we were grateful for and share one value. I always believed that practicing being grateful on a daily basis brought genuine happiness. And I also thought it was never too early to teach the kids about values. I figured as they grew older they could navigate their relationships better if they knew what they valued and aligned it with future friends and potential partners.

After we all sit down to eat and take a few bites of our food, I'll say, "Who wants to go first saying their Gratefuls?" Surprisingly, this has always made for easy conversation. You get to know a lot about your kids when you hear what they are grateful for. Sometimes it was as simple as chocolate milk. Other times it was deeper, like having access to a healthy meal, "because in some places, kids don't have enough food". At times, they became grateful for the same things I said I was grateful for, which always made me proud and brought us closer.

There was so much I learned about parenting and about myself. If I could have given myself some advice when I first started this adventure, it would have been: *Let it go.*

Let go of high standards. Mark, the kids, and YOU will never measure up to these ideals you have in your head. You have to share space and time with four other human beings who all have their own way of doing things and a different set of standards. You need to accept that. Be gentler with yourself.

Let go of the idea of having a showroom-ready home. Hell, just be happy if the place gets vacuumed regularly! There will be shoes, empty toilet paper rolls, toys, and all sorts of items that are laying in the middle of the floor for no good reason. Just walk over them and leave a note on the fridge asking everyone to pick up their stuff while you are at work. And then expect half of the stuff to still be on the floor when you come home. Accept some of the mess and focus on having a happy home instead.

Let go of the idea that it will be like this forever. *It will not be like this forever.* The kids will grow up and move out one day. Keep your relationship with Mark strong throughout all the chaos. You have the ability to create and recognize fun snapshots along this entire journey. Keep your sense of humour.

Let the stress go by eating healthy food and meditating regularly. Go on that hike. Take that trip to Mexico. Oh, and don't drink so much wine.

I'm grateful for the kids.

I'm grateful for Mark.

I'm grateful for how I've tried my best.

And I value this family.

# Acknowledgements

A huge thank you to Mark and the kids for making this crazy story possible, and for letting me tell it. Mark, I know you rather I had spent the time with you instead of countless hours at the computer writing this book, so thank you for your patience. It's finally finished! I look forward to more tales as we grow together. Plus, I need new material for my next book.

Thanks to my brother and sister who confirmed childhood details, and my wonderful mom who has been my cheerleader throughout this process.

To my friends and family members who I wrote about: you are not simply characters in this book, you are important to me and I am grateful for all of you. Thank you for teaching me life lessons and letting me share these stories.

This book would not exist in this form if it hadn't been for Myrl Coulter and her words of wisdom and guidance. Thank you for mentoring me on this journey. You opened up my writing by asking the right questions and I'll always remember the most important thing you told me: "Write better words."

Heartfelt thanks to my early readers and best friends: Stacy Boone, April Wells, and Darlene Fontaine. You all encouraged me and gave me honest feedback with endless love and support.

Thank you to Kimmy Beach for copy-editing my manuscript and brainstorming new ideas with me.

To Alecia and Carlos at Schreyer Urbina Photography, thank you for creating some white magic with your time and vision. And thank you Danielle Sweetnam for your mad make-up skills.

And last, but by no means least, thank you to Nakita Valerio who offered me a fresh set of eyes when I lost perspective. Your copy-editing and comments changed the final manuscript for the better. Thank you for convincing me to add back the chapter that I had cut. You are a true friend.

Lightning Source UK Ltd.
Milton Keynes UK
UKHW041841251119
354234UK00004B/96/P